Elegant
DESSERTS

Elegant DESSERTS

HPBooks®

P.O. Box 5367, Tucson, AZ 85703
602/888-2150
ISBN 0-89586-350-2
Library of Congress Catalog Card Number 84-81092
© 1984 HPBooks, Inc. Printed in Italy
Cover photo: Snow Cake, pages 14-15

ANOTHER BEST-SELLING VOLUME FROM HPBooks®

Publisher: Rick Bailey
Editorial Director: Retha M. Davis
Editors: Retha M. Davis, Carroll Latham
Art Director: Don Burton
Book Assembly: Kathleen Koopman
Typography: Cindy Coatsworth, Michelle Claridge

Translated by Caroline Beamish

© 1981 Shogakukan Publishing Co. Ltd., Tokyo for the original edition

English translation copyright © 1984 Arnoldo Mondadori Editore S.p.A., Milan

First published under the title *I Dolci*, 1983

Arnoldo Mondadori Editore S.p.A., Milan for the international edition

Cover photo credit: Rick Gayle Studio, Phoenix, Arizona

CONTENTS

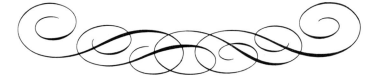

To Delight the Eye & Please the Palate

This attractive book is a gourmet's delight. It includes internationally famous cakes, puddings, molds, mousses, soufflés, cookies and other desserts. The recipes in this collection include masterpieces developed over centuries. Also included are other products which, strictly speaking, are not desserts. These include cheesecakes, scones, brioches and croissants to accompany ice cream or to serve with coffee or tea.

The pastry cook, confectioner and ice-cream maker welcome new trends in their art. At the same time they are intent on preserving traditional methods and practices. They insist the decoration of the finished product is of supreme importance, whether traditional or modern. Piped-icing flowers and candied fruit are specially manufactured for decorating cakes and pastries. A wide variety of tiny masterpieces in pastry, praline or marzipan—in their finely pleated paper cases—tempt both the eye and the palate. Rosettes, stars, scrolls and flourishes are patiently reproduced to delight the eye.

In comparison, the art of making desserts is on a slightly different and more modest scale. Desserts are intended to be eaten immediately. The flavor of the dessert must harmonize with and complement the courses that have preceded it. It must be an integral part of the whole meal. Some desserts are exceptionally light and frothy. Others are substantial and extremely filling.

The visual element is often a matter of secondary importance. Often, a dessert will consist of something baked and served in the same dish. Or it may be individual servings of zabaglione or mousse, whipped up at the last minute. None of these requires elaborate decoration—perhaps just a dollop of whipped cream. Ice creams, sherbets and sorbets can be served simply with a wafer or cookie. Creams and gâteaux are more fashionable than ever and make a fitting end to any meal.

Thanks to modern transportation, the most exotic varieties of fruit are widely available, providing a complement to seasonal home-grown fruit. Fruit can be transformed into delicate jellies, mousses and sorbets. It can be combined with other fruits, providing cooks with new and unusual flavors. Fruit purees can be used as sauces for creams and mousses, or can be mixed with liqueurs and served with fruit salads and ice creams. Fruit is the basis for syrups, juices, jellies and jams.

Recipes and methods for making basic pastries and doughs have remained more or less unchanged over the years. Follow recipe directions and measure ingredients exactly for the best results. Do this even though the emphasis today may seem to point toward the importance of decorative techniques and the actual presentation of the finished creation. For basic cookery information, see page 187.

All decorations are designed to have visual appeal. Of greater importance are flavor and texture, which can only be perfected if the recipe is followed exactly and the ingredients measured with the greatest care. Some pastries should be crisp, some flaky. Some should melt in the mouth. Others must be firm enough to be filled with custard or whipped cream. Recipes are designed to meet these needs.

Use only the ingredients suggested in the recipe unless something is unobtainable. Cutting corners for reasons of economy—using margarine in place of butter or imitation sour cream instead of real cream—rarely works where desserts are concerned. Fresh butter, cream, best-quality flour, sugar, walnuts and almonds are essential ingredients to keep on hand.

In housewares specialty stores, you'll find molds and special utensils for the most complex creations. You'll find candy and deep-fat thermometers, molds and pans in all shapes and sizes, wire racks on which tiny sweets can be covered with chocolate and smaller molds in a variety of shapes for making cold desserts. You'll find molds made specially for jellied sweets, fondants, marzipan figures and petits fours.

What is valid for the professional chef or confectioner is also valid for the amateur cook. Just as the professional has customers to satisfy, so the home cook must live up to the expectations of family and friends and create a good impression on guests. The extra effort will be greatly rewarded.

Whether you use this book for entertaining friends or to make a special treat for the family, you will produce desserts to be proud of.

Arne Krüger

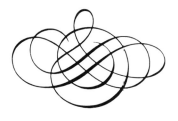

CAKES & DESSERTS FOR SPECIAL OCCASIONS

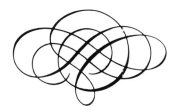

Coffee-Butter-Cream Cake

Sponge Cake: 3 eggs, separated ● 1/2 cup sugar ● 1 tablespoon orange liqueur or orange juice ●
1/2 teaspoon vanilla extract ● 1 cup all-purpose flour ● 2 tablespoons butter, melted, cooled   **Raspberry Filling:**
1/4 cup seedless raspberry jam ● 1-1/2 tablespoons lemon juice   **Coffee Butter Cream:** 3/4 cup butter, room temperature ●
1/2 cup powdered sugar ● 2 egg yolks ● 1 egg white, if desired ●
1 tablespoon instant coffee dissolved in 1/4 cup boiling water, cooled, or 1/4 cup very strong coffee
Chantilly Cream, page 195   **Decoration:** 1/2 cup chocolate curls or flakes

1. For the cake, preheat oven to 375F (190C). Grease and flour an 8-inch springform pan. Beat egg yolks and sugar over hot water until mixture is almost white and ribbons form when beater is lifted, 5 to 8 minutes with an electric mixer. Remove from heat. Add orange liqueur or orange juice and vanilla.

2. Beat egg whites until stiff but not dry. Fold 1/2 the egg whites into egg-yolk mixture. Sift 1/2 the flour over batter; fold in. Fold in 1/2 the remaining egg whites and remaining flour. Then fold in remaining egg whites, being careful not to deflate egg whites. Quickly fold in melted butter. Immediately pour into prepared pan.

3. Bake 35 to 40 minutes. Cool in pan 10 minutes; then turn out on a wire rack to completely cool. Cut into 3 equal layers.

4. For the filling, combine jam and lemon juice. If seedless jam is not available, press mixture through a sieve to remove seeds.

5. For the butter cream, beat together butter, sugar, egg yolks and egg white, if desired, until blended. Added egg white will make a softer, fluffier frosting. Slowly beat in coffee. If frosting is too soft for spreading, refrigerate until of spreading consistency.

6. To assemble cake, spread 1/2 the filling on 1 sponge layer. Spread 1/2 the Chantilly Cream over filling. Cover first sponge layer with second layer; repeat layers of filling and Chantilly Cream using

remainder of each. Cover with third sponge layer. Spread cake with 3/4 of Coffee Butter Cream. Using a piping bag fitted with a round tip, decorate cake with remaining butter cream. Sprinkle with chocolate. Makes 1 (8-inch) cake.

Snow Cake

Sponge Cake, page 18   **Custard:** 1-1/2 cups milk • 1/2 cup powdered sugar • 1 tablespoon all-purpose flour •
1 tablespoon cornstarch • 2 egg yolks • 1 tablespoon butter • 4-1/2 to 6 tablespoons brandy   **Chantilly Cream,** page 195,
double recipe

1. Prepare Sponge Cake, steps
1-4, page 19. For custard,
scald milk over low heat.
Combine sugar, flour and
cornstarch. Gradually add to
milk, stirring constantly. Stir
together until thickened.

2. In a small bowl, beat egg
yolks. Add small amount of
milk mixture to egg yolks.
Then add egg-yolk mixture to
remaining milk mixture.

3. Stir over medium heat until
thickened.

4. Add butter; stir until
melted. Cool custard. To
prevent a skin from forming
on surface of custard, cover
with plastic wrap. Cool until
ready to use.

5. Cut cooled cake into 3
equal layers. Sprinkle cake
layers with 1-1/2 to 2
tablespoons brandy per layer.
Spread 1/2 the custard on 1
layer. Top with a second layer.
Cover with remaining
custard. Top with remaining
layer.

6. Chantilly Cream must be
very stiff to pipe. Cover entire
cake with Chantilly Cream.
Use a piping bag to decorate
cake with Chantilly Cream, as
desired. Butter Cream or
Royal Icing, page 195, may be
substituted for Chantilly
Cream, if desired. Makes 1
(8-inch) cake.

Strawberry-Cream Gâteau

1 (8-inch) Sponge Cake, page 18 ● 3 tablespoons Grand Marnier or maraschino liqueur ● Chantilly Cream, page 195 ●
3 cups strawberries

1. Prepare Sponge Cake, steps 1-4, page 19. Cool; cut into 3 equal layers. Sprinkle each layer with liqueur.

2. Prepare Chantilly Cream. Cut 1 cup strawberries in halves.

3. Spread bottom layer of cake with 1/2 cup Chantilly Cream. Top with half of sliced strawberries.

4. Place middle cake layer over bottom layer. Spread with 1/2 cup Chantilly Cream and remaining halved strawberries. Top with final cake layer.

5. Reserve 1 cup Chantilly Cream for decoration. Spread remaining Chantilly Cream over top and side of cake. Decorate with reserved Chantilly Cream and remaining strawberries. Makes 1 (8-inch) cake.

Prince Leopold Cake

Chocolate Cake: 6 tablespoons butter, room temperature • 3/4 cup sugar • 8 eggs, separated •
1-1/2 cups ground almonds • 7 oz. baking chocolate, grated • 3/4 cup all-purpose flour • 3 tablespoons rum
Chocolate Frosting: 1 cup whipping cream • 7 oz. semisweet chocolate • 1/2 cup powdered sugar •
1 teaspoon vanilla extract

1. For cake, preheat oven to 375F (190C). Grease and flour a 9-inch springform pan. In a large bowl, cream together butter and sugar. Beat in egg yolks, 1 at a time. Stir in almonds, chocolate, flour and rum. In a medium bowl, beat egg whites until stiff but not dry. Stir 1/4 of beaten egg whites into batter. Carefully fold in remaining egg whites.

2. Pour batter into prepared pan. Bake 40 to 45 minutes or until cake tests done. Remove from oven. Cool in pan 10 minutes. Remove from pan and cool on a wire rack. When completely cool, split cake into 2 equal layers.

3. For frosting, combine cream and 5 ounces chocolate. Cook over medium heat until chocolate melts and mixture begins to boil. Stir well. Refrigerate until slightly warm. Beat until smooth. Beat in powdered sugar and vanilla.

4. To assemble cake, place bottom layer on a plate. Top with 1/3 of the frosting. Top with remaining layer. Spread remaining frosting over side and top of cake.

5. Coarsely grate remaining 2 ounces chocolate. Sprinkle chocolate over top and side of cake. Makes 1 (9-inch) cake.

TIP: For a sweeter taste, additional powdered sugar may be added to the frosting.

Coffee-Almond Cake

Sponge Cake: 3/4 cup sugar ● 6 eggs, separated ● 1/4 teaspoon vanilla extract ● 1-1/2 cups sifted cake flour ● Coffee liqueur to soak cake **Coffee Butter Cream,** page 13 **Decoration:** 1/2 cup toasted flaked almonds ● 1 tablespoon unsweetened cocoa powder or chocolate drink mix

1. For cake, preheat oven to 325F (165C). Butter and flour an 3-inch springform pan. Beat together sugar, egg yolks and vanilla over a bowl of hot water.

2. Beat egg whites until stiff but not dry; fold gently into sugar mixture.

3. Sift flour; fold into mixture.

4. Pour batter into prepared pan. Bake 40 minutes or until cake tests done.

5. For butter cream, follow method on page 13. Or, make Glacé Icing, page 195, using 1 cup sugar. Then gradually add to egg yolks.

6. Cream the butter; stir into egg-yolk mixture. Blend in coffee.

7. Cut cake into 3 equal layers. Using a pastry brush, brush layers lightly with coffee liqueur. Spread each layer with Coffee Butter Cream. Cover entire cake with remaining butter cream.

8. Press almonds around side of cake. Place 1/2-inch-wide paper strips diagonally across cake in a lattice pattern. Sieve cocoa powder or drink mix over cake. Remove paper strips carefully. Makes 1 (8-inch) cake.

Chocolate-Mousse Cake

Cake: 3 eggs ● 1/2 cup sugar ● 1/4 cup unsweetened cocoa powder ● 3 tablespoons hot water ● 3 tablespoons butter, melted ● 1/2 cup all-purpose flour **Mousse:** 3 egg whites ● 3/4 cup plus 2 tablespoons sugar ● 1/3 cup water ● 2 tablespoons kirsch ● 1/2 cup sugar ● 6 tablespoons butter ● 1 egg ● 1 egg yolk ● 1-1/2 oz. semisweet chocolate, melted **Kirsch Syrup:** 1/3 cup sugar ● 1/3 cup water ● 1/3 cup kirsch **Decoration:** Milk chocolate flakes

1. For cake, preheat oven to 350F (175C). Grease and flour an 8-inch springform pan. Beat eggs and sugar together until pale.

2. In a separate bowl, combine cocoa, water and butter; blend well.

3. Sift flour slowly into egg mixture. Beat well.

4. Add cocoa mixture from step 2; stir until blended. Pour batter into prepared pan. Bake 20 minutes or until cake tests done.

5. Remove from pan. Cover with a damp cloth to keep cake soft.

6. For mousse, beat 3 egg whites until stiff but not dry. Boil together 3/4 cup plus 2 tablespoons sugar, water and kirsch to hard-ball stage (250-266F, 121-130C). Pour in a thin stream over beaten egg whites, beating constantly until cool.

7. In a large bowl, beat together 1/2 cup sugar, butter, 1 egg, egg yolk and chocolate; blend well. Fold chocolate mixture into mixture from step 6. Refrigerate until ready to use.

8. Cut cake into 2 equal layers. For Kirsch Syrup, combine sugar, water and kirsch. Cook to thread stage (230-234F, 110-112C). Brush bottom layer with hot Kirsch Syrup. When cool, spread this layer with mousse mixture. Place second layer on top. Cover entire cake with mousse. Refrigerate immediately to firm the mousse. Decorate with chocolate flakes after mousse is firm. Refrigerate until ready to serve. Makes 1 (8-inch) cake.

Diplomat

2 (9-inch) squares Puff Pastry or Flaky Pastry, page 196 ● 1 (8- or 10-inch-square) Sponge Cake, 1-1/2 inches thick, page 196 ●
1-1/4 cups Rum Butter Cream, see Liqueur Butter Cream, page 195 ● Maraschino liqueur ● 1/4 cup powdered sugar

1. Prepare Puff Pastry or Flaky Pastry and Sponge Cake.

2. Place 1 pastry square on a flat serving dish or tray.

3. Spread 1/2 of Rum Butter Cream over pastry.

4. Cut cake to fit over top of pastry. Cut pieces to fit, if necessary to make an even layer. Brush with generous amount of liqueur.

5. Spread with remaining Rum Butter Cream.

6. Cover with remaining pastry square. Dust with powdered sugar.

7. Use a pastry wheel to make a decorative design in powdered sugar. Makes 8 to 10 servings.

Mille-Feuille Gâteau

Zabaglione Cream, page 195 ● 4 (8-inch) circles Flaky Pastry, page 196 ● 2 Ladyfingers, page 131, or other ladyfingers, crumbled ● 1 cup finely chopped toasted blanched hazelnuts or almonds ● Powdered sugar ● Chantilly Cream, page 195 ● Candied cherries

1. Prepare Zabaglione Cream.

2. Place 1 pastry circle on a serving dish. Top with 1/4 of Zabaglione Cream; spread to edges.

3. Repeat with remaining pastry circles, topping each with 1/4 of Zabaglione Cream.

4. Combine crumbled ladyfingers and chopped nuts. Sprinkle over top layer of gâteau.

5. Dust with powdered sugar.

6. Decorate with rosettes of Chantilly Cream. On each rosette, place a candied cherry.

7. Refrigerate until ready to serve. Makes 6 to 8 servings.

Christmas Cake

Almond Sponge: 6 eggs, separated • 1/2 cup sugar • 1 teaspoon almond extract • 1/2 cup all-purpose flour • 1/4 cup ground almonds   **Grand Marnier Syrup:** 1/4 cup sugar • 3 tablespoons water • 1/4 cup Grand Marnier
Grand Marnier Butter Cream: 3/4 cup butter or margarine, room temperature • 1/2 cup powdered sugar • 2 egg yolks • 1/4 cup Grand Marnier • 1/2 cup toasted pistachios, finely ground • Green food coloring
Decoration: White, yellow and chocolate Marzipan, page 193 • Royal Icing, page 195 • Chocolate Icing, see Glacé Icing, page 195

1. For cake, grease and flour a 9-inch springform pan. Preheat oven to 375F (190C). Beat egg yolks and sugar over hot water until almost white in color and ribbons form when beater is lifted, 5 to 8 minutes with an electric mixer. Remove from heat; stir in almond extract. Beat egg whites until stiff but not dry. Fold 1/4 of beaten egg whites into egg-yolk mixture. Combine flour and ground almonds. Sift 1/2 the flour mixture over batter; fold in. Fold in 1/2 the remaining egg whites and all of remaining flour mixture. Carefully fold in remaining egg whites. Pour batter into prepared pan. Bake about 35 minutes. Cool in pan 10 minutes. Then turn out onto a wire rack to cool completely. Split cake into 2 layers.

To make syrup, dissolve sugar in water in a small saucepan over medium heat. Bring to a boil; boil about 2 minutes. Cool. Stir in Grand Marnier. Sprinkle lower layer of cake with cool syrup.

2. To make butter cream, in a large bowl, beat together butter or margarine, sugar and egg yolks until well blended. Gradually beat in Grand Marnier. Beat in pistachios. Add coloring, drop by drop, until desired color is achieved. If frosting is too soft, refrigerate to desired spreading consistency.

3. Spread 1 layer of cake with butter cream. Place top layer of cake on lower layer. Cover entire cake with remaining butter cream.

4. Decorate top of cake with a candle made from white marzipan, stars made from yellow marzipan and a candlestick made from chocolate marzipan.

5. To decorate, make 2 paper icing nozzles or use a piping bag with a fine plain writing tip.

6. Decorate cake with Royal Icing and Chocolate Icing.

TIP: The decoration of this cake can be varied to suit any occasion.

Trifle with Nuts

1 (8-inch) layer Sponge Cake, about 1 inch thick, page 196 • Kirsch, maraschino or curaçao liqueur •
1-1/2 cups Cream Custard, page 194 • Toasted nuts, page 190 • 1-1/2 cups Chantilly Cream, page 195

1. Place cake layer in a round, 9-inch glass dish, 2-1/2 to 3 inches deep.

2. Using a pastry brush, brush cake with liqueur.

3. Spread with custard. Layer will be about 1/2 inch thick.

4. Decorate with toasted nuts.

5. Place trifle, plates, spoons or forks in freezer at least 30 minutes.

6. Before serving, decorate with Chantilly Cream. Makes about 6 servings.

Sachertorte

1-1/4 cups sugar ● 2/3 cup butter, room temperature ● 6 eggs, separated ● 5 oz. unsweetened or semisweet chocolate, melted, cooled ● 3/4 cup ground toasted blanched almonds ● 1 teaspoon vanilla extract ● 1 cup all-purpose flour ● 1/4 cup milk ● 1/2 cup fine breadcrumbs ● 1/2 cup rum or kirsch ● 1/4 cup apricot jam, sieved ● Chocolate Frosting, page 17

1. Preheat oven to 375F (190C). Grease and flour a 9-inch springform pan.

2. In a medium bowl, cream sugar with butter. Beat in egg yolks, 1 at a time. Stir in chocolate, almonds and vanilla. Stir in 1/2 the flour alternately with 1/2 the milk. Blend well. Beat in remaining flour and milk. Beat egg whites until stiff peaks form. Stir breadcrumbs and 1/4 of the beaten egg whites into chocolate mixture. Fold in remaining egg whites.

3. Pour into prepared pan. Bake 35 to 40 minutes or until cake tests done. Remove from oven. Cool in pan 10 minutes. Then remove from pan and cool on a wire rack several hours. Split cake into 3 equal layers.

4. To assemble cake, position bottom layer on a serving plate. Sprinkle with 1/2 the rum or kirsch; spread lightly with 1/3 the jam. Top with second layer. Repeat process with liqueur and jam. Cover 2 layers with top layer. Spread with remaining jam. Cover entire cake with frosting. Use a fork to achieve rough texture on cake's surface. Makes 1 (9-inch) cake.

Sachertorte was created over a century ago for Prince Metternich by his cook, Franz Sacher. Since then, it has become famous all over the world. The "original" recipe is a jealously guarded secret of the hotel and restaurant of the Sacher family in Vienna.

Coffee & Brandy Cake

Cake: 6 eggs • 1 cup sugar • 1-1/2 cups all-purpose flour • 1/4 cup butter or margarine • 1/4 cup instant coffee powder • 2 tablespoons brandy **Cream Filling:** 2 egg yolks • 3/4 cup granulated sugar • 1/4 cup all-purpose flour • 3/4 cup milk • 1 tablespoon powdered sugar • 1/2 cup whipping cream, whipped • 2 tablespoons instant-coffee powder • 2 tablespoons brandy **Decoration:** 1-1/2 cups Chantilly Cream, page 195 • Marzipan, page 193

The leaf decoration on this cake is made of marzipan which you can make yourself or purchase commercially. The final decoration is a matter of personal taste.

1. For the cake, preheat oven to 325F (165C). In a large bowl over hot water, beat eggs and sugar 8 to 10 minutes.

2. Gradually fold in flour.

3. Melt butter or margarine in a small saucepan. Dissolve coffee in brandy. Blend melted butter or margarine and coffee mixture together. Stir into cake mixture.

4. Line a deep 8-inch cake pan with waxed paper or buttered parchment paper. Pour in cake mixture. Bake 30 minutes or until cake tests done. Cool in pan 10 minutes. Then turn out onto a wire rack. Cut cake into 3 or 4 equal layers.

5. To make cream filling, beat egg yolks, gradually beating in granulated sugar. Gradually beat in flour.

6. Warm milk slightly. Gradually add warm milk to egg mixture. Pour into a medium saucepan.

7. Place over low heat. Cook, stirring constantly, until mixture thickens, 6 to 8 minutes. Let cool. If necessary, refrigerate until cool.

8. Stir in powdered sugar. Carefully fold in whipped cream. Fold in coffee, dissolved in brandy. Spread filling between cake layers. Cover entire cake with Chantilly Cream. Use a spatula to spread smoothly. Using a piping bag and various tips, decorate cake with remaining Chantilly Cream. Makes 1 (8-inch) cake.

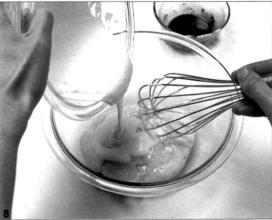

Cassata Siciliana

Cassata: 4 cups ricotta cheese (2 lbs.) • 1 cup sugar • 1/2 cup water • 1/2 teaspoon ground cinnamon • 5 oz. baking chocolate, coarsely grated • 1-1/2 cups finely chopped candied lemon peel • 1/4 cup pistachios • 1/2 cup Marsala • 1 (10-inch) Sponge Cake, page 196 • 1/2 to 1 cup maraschino liqueur
Lemon Icing: 3 cups powdered sugar • 1/4 cup strained lemon juice • Green food coloring • Blue food coloring
Decoration: Several large strips of candied lemon peel • Candied cherries

1. For Cassata, line a 9- or 10-inch high-sided pan or a bowl with rounded bottom with plastic wrap.

2. In a medium bowl, beat ricotta cheese until smooth.

3. In a saucepan, heat sugar with 1/2 cup water until you have a clear syrup. Pour syrup over ricotta cheese; blend in cinnamon. Cool to room temperature.

4. Add chocolate, candied lemon peel, pistachios and Marsala.

5. Cut sponge cake into fingers. Using only enough cake fingers to line pan or bowl, dip cake in maraschino liqueur. Line pan or bowl with maraschino-dipped cake.

6. Pour ricotta mixture into cake-lined pan. Cover with remaining cake fingers but do not dip in liqueur. Refrigerate 4 to 5 hours.

7. For Lemon Icing, combine sugar and lemon juice. Add more juice if icing is too thick to spread. Tint to desired color with about 2 parts blue to 1 part green food coloring. Start with small amounts of color.

8. Turn out cassata. Cover with Lemon Icing. Decorate with candied-lemon-peel strips and candied cherries. Makes 1 (9- or 10-inch) Cassata.

Cassata Siciliana is a cake, not to be confused with the frozen Cassata alla Siciliana, which is an ice-cream dessert.

Zuccotto

1 (10-inch) Sponge Cake, page 196 ● 1/4 cup cognac or brandy ● 1/4 cup rum ● 1/4 cup kirsch ●
3-1/2 cups whipping cream ● 1 cup powdered sugar ● 3/4 cup chopped candied fruit ● 2 or 3 dark sweet cherries, pitted ●
3/4 cup ground toasted almonds ● 3/4 cup ground toasted hazelnuts ● 3 to 4 oz. semisweet chocolate, finely grated
Decoration: Unsweetened cocoa powder or chocolate drink mix ● Powdered sugar

1. Cut cake into 1/3- to 1/2-inch-thick slices; then cut into strips to fit a 3-quart mold or bowl. Combine cognac or brandy, rum and kirsch. Sprinkle 3/4 the cake strips with liqueur mixture. Line a 3-quart mold or bowl with liqueur-sprinkled strips, trimming cake to fit.

2. Beat 1-3/4 cups whipping cream with 1/2 cup powdered sugar. Fold in candied fruit. Pour into cake-lined mold. Position cherries in center. Refrigerate.

3. Beat remaining 1-3/4 cups whipping cream with remaining 1/2 cup powdered sugar. Fold in ground nuts and grated chocolate. Pour mixture into mold.

4. Top the cream with remaining cake slices that have not been sprinkled with liqueur mixture. Trim to fit as needed.

5. Refrigerate at least 2 hours.

6. Unmold on a serving dish. Decorate with sifted cocoa or drink mix and powdered sugar as shown. Makes 1 large zuccotto.

Walnut Charlotte

30 Ladyfingers, page 131, or other ladyfingers ● 1/2 cup or more kirsch or other liqueur ● 1 generous cup butter ●
2 generous cups powdered sugar ● 2 eggs, separated ● 1-1/4 cups ground walnuts ● 1-1/2 to 2 cups Chantilly Cream,
page 195 ● 1/2 cup candied cherries ● 1/2 cup walnut halves

1. Dip ladyfingers in liqueur. Reserve about 8 dipped ladyfingers for top. Use remaining ladyfingers to line base and side of a 7-inch charlotte mold or a deep 7-inch springform pan.

2. In a medium bowl, cream butter and sugar until light and fluffy. Beat in egg yolks, 1 at a time. Stir in ground nuts. Beat egg whites until stiff but not dry; fold into butter mixture.

3. Pour butter mixture into mold. Cover with reserved ladyfingers. Refrigerate several hours.

4. To serve, unmold onto a serving dish; decorate with Chantilly Cream, candied cherries and walnut halves. Makes 6 to 8 servings.

A charlotte is a French dessert made with ladyfingers or *boudoir biscuits* that are dipped in liqueur and used to line the base and sides of a mold. When it is turned out on a serving dish, the ladyfingers form an outer shell that is then covered with Chantilly Cream. A charlotte mold is round, with a 7-inch diameter, and is about 4 inches deep. A charlotte may also be filled with Bavarian cream.

Gâteau Saint Honoré

1 (10-inch) Sponge Cake, page 196 ● 16 Profiteroles, page 58, without chocolate glaze ● 3 cups Cream Custard or Pastry Cream, page 194 ● 1/4 cup maraschino liqueur ● 1/4 cup sherry ● 1-1/2 cups Chantilly Cream, page 195 ● 3 or 4 Ladyfingers, page 131, or other ladyfingers, crumbled ● 1/4 cup sugar ● 1 tablespoon honey ● 2 tablespoons water ● 1 cup Saint-Honoré Cream, page 194 ● 1 cup Chocolate Saint-Honoré Cream, page 194

1. Prepare Sponge Cake. Cool; cut into 2 equal layers.

2. Prepare Profiteroles. Use a fine tip and a pastry bag to fill Profiteroles with Cream Custard or Pastry Cream. Reserve remaining custard or cream.

3. Place 1 cake layer on a flat serving dish. Combine liqueur and sherry; sprinkle 1/2 over cake layer.

4. Stir 2 to 3 tablespoons Chantilly Cream into reserved custard or cream.

Spread 1/2 of custard or cream mixture over cake layer on serving dish.

5. Top with remaining cake layer; sprinkle with remaining liqueur mixture.

6. Spread remaining custard or cream mixture over top. Sprinkle with crumbled ladyfingers.

7. In a small saucepan, combine sugar, honey and water. Stir over low heat until sugar and honey dissolve. Use to brush over filled Profiteroles.

8. Use a pastry bag and tips to decorate top of cake with alternate rows of vanilla and chocolate Saint-Honoré Cream. Arrange filled Profiteroles around edge. Separate with piped Chantilly Cream. Makes 8 to 10 servings.

This is a variation of the classic Gâteau Saint Honoré which has a base of sweet shortcrust pastry. Saint Honoré was the Bishop of Amiens in northwest France in the 7th century. He is now the patron saint of pastry cooks.

Strawberry & Chestnut Tart

Sweet Shortcrust Pastry: 1-1/4 cups all-purpose flour ● 5 tablespoons butter or margarine ● 1/2 cup sugar ● 1 egg ●
1 teaspoon vanilla extract   **Chestnut Filling:** 1/2 lb. cooked chestnuts (about 2-1/4 cups sieved) ●
6 tablespoons butter or margarine ● 3/4 cup granulated sugar ● 1/2 cup half and half ● 2 egg yolks ●
1/2 cup whipping cream ● 1/4 cup powdered sugar   **Chestnut Topping, if desired:** 1/2 lb. cooked chestnuts,
pureed (about 2-1/4 cups) ● 1/2 teaspoon salt ● 6 tablespoons powdered sugar ● 1 tablespoon kirsch
Decoration: 25 to 30 strawberries, washed, hulled ● 1/4 cup apricot jam

To prepare chestnuts for use in filling and topping for this tart,
cut a slit in the shell of each chestnut. Place chestnuts in a pan
pierced with holes. Roast them over a flame until their skins split
and come off easily. Remove shells and skins. Boil chestnuts in
milk to cover, adding 1 teaspoon salt to each 1 pint of milk.
When chestnuts are tender, drain well. If you cannot roast
chestnuts first, you can boil them with their skins on but they
will take longer to cook.

1. Preheat oven to 350F (175C). Prepare pastry using method on page 39. Roll out pastry to about 1/8 inch thick. Line a 9-inch flan pan with removable bottom.

2. Press pastry firmly to side of flan pan without stretching.

3. Trim excess pastry. Prick pastry shell with a fork.

4. For filling, sieve chestnuts.

5. In a medium bowl, cream butter or margarine. Add sugar; blend well. Blend in half and half.

6. Stir in sieved chestnuts and egg yolks.

7. Pour chestnut mixture into pastry shell. Bake 25 to 30 minutes. Cool completely. Remove from pan.

8. In a large bowl, whip the whipping cream. Fold in powdered sugar. Spread mixture evenly over tart. Arrange strawberries around edge of tart. Warm apricot jam over low heat until thin enough to drizzle. Drizzle jam over strawberries. If preparing chestnut topping, sieve chestnuts. Blend in salt, sugar and kirsch. Fill a piping bag with chestnut mixture. Decorate top of flan with mixture. Chestnut puree for topping may be darker than shown in photo.

Ricotta Cheesecake

Sweet Shortcrust Pastry: 2 cups plus 2 tablespoons all-purpose flour ● 3/4 cup sugar ● 3/4 cup butter ● 1 egg ●
2 egg yolks   **Cheese Filling:** 3 cups ricotta cheese (24 oz.) ● 2-1/2 cups powdered sugar ● 1 egg ● 3 egg yolks ●
2 teaspoons grated orange peel ● 1/2 teaspoon ground cinnamon   **Meringue:** 5 egg whites ●
2 cups powdered sugar, sifted

1. Prepare pastry as directed on page 39. Press into bottom and side of a 10-inch springform pan.

2. Preheat oven to 375F (190C).

3. For filling, in a large bowl, beat together cheese, sugar, egg, egg yolks, orange peel and cinnamon.

4. Pour cheese mixture into pastry-lined pan.

5. Bake 35 to 40 minutes or until firmly set. Remove from oven. Turn off oven heat.

6. For meringue, beat egg whites until stiff but not dry. Fold in powdered sugar, 1/2 cup at a time. Spread 1/2 the meringue over cheesecake. Decorate with additional meringue using a piping bag. Return cheesecake to warm oven. Let sit in oven 30 to 40 minutes to set meringue.
Makes 1 (10-inch) cheesecake.

Quick Apple Cake

6 cooking apples • Juice of 1/2 lemon • 1/4 cup sugar   **Cake:** 1/4 cup butter or margarine • 1/2 cup sugar •
2 egg yolks • Juice of 1/2 lemon • Grated peel of 1/2 lemon • 1 cup all-purpose flour • 1 teaspoon baking powder •
6 tablespoons milk • 3 tablespoons rum • 3 egg whites   **Glaze:** 2 tablespoons butter or margarine, melted •
1 egg yolk   **Decoration:** Powdered sugar, if desired

1. Preheat oven to 375F (190C). Butter a 1-1/2- to 2-quart baking dish.

2. Peel and core apples. Sprinkle apples with juice of 1/2 lemon and 1/4 cup sugar.

3. For cake, cream 1/4 cup butter or margarine and 1/2 cup sugar. Beat in egg yolks, juice of 1/2 lemon and lemon peel.

4. Sift flour and baking powder together; add to the mixture along with milk and rum. Stir until blended.

5. Beat egg whites until light and fluffy; fold carefully into batter.

6. Pour batter into buttered dish. Press apples into mixture. For the glaze, combine melted butter or margarine and egg yolk. Brush or drizzle cake with glaze.

7. Bake 40 to 50 minutes. Remove from oven; sprinkle with powdered sugar, if desired. Makes 1 cake.

Apple Pie

Sweet Shortcrust Pastry: 2 cups all-purpose flour • 1/2 cup sugar • 1/2 teaspoon salt • 1/2 cup butter • 2 egg yolks
Apple Filling: 2 lbs. cooking apples, 7 to 8 medium • 1 teaspoon lemon juice • 1 large lemon slice • 2/3 to 3/4 cup sugar •
1/4 teaspoon ground nutmeg • 1/2 teaspoon ground cinnamon • 2 tablespoons all-purpose flour • 2 tablespoons orange juice
Glaze: 1 to 2 eggs, beaten

1. In a medium bowl, combine flour, sugar and salt. Work in butter with your fingertips.

2. Add egg yolks, blending as quickly as possible. Continue to work pastry on a floured surface using a spatula until blended.

3. Roll out pastry fairly thick.

4. Lift pastry frequently on the rolling pin. Dust pastry with flour so it does not stick.

5. Fold pastry into thirds.

6. Roll out pastry again fairly thick.

Continued on next page.

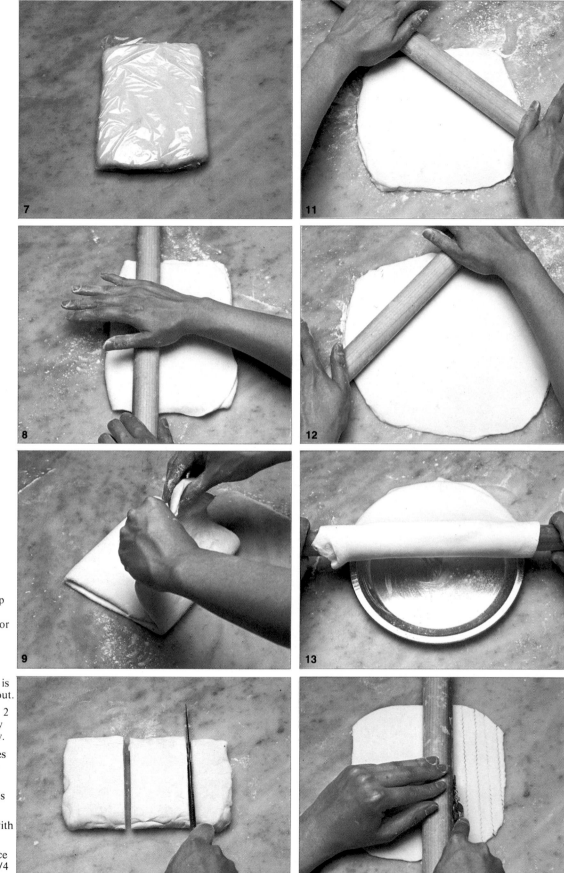

7. Fold in thirds again. Wrap in plastic wrap or a damp cloth. Leave in a cool place or refrigerate 30 minutes.

8. Roll out pastry again.

9. Fold in thirds to form a rectangle, being sure that it is an even thickness throughout.

10. Cut pastry into 3 pieces, 2 pieces each 2/5 of the pastry and 1 piece 1/5 of the pastry.

11. Roll 1 of the larger pieces of pastry out from center to side.

12. Roll pastry to a thickness of 1/4 inch.

13. Line a 9-inch pie plate with rolled pastry.

14. Roll out the smaller piece of pastry to a thickness of 1/4 inch. Using a pastry wheel, cut into 1/2-inch-wide strips.

15. Feel and core apples; cut into large slices. Immerse in a mixture of 1 quart water and 3 tablespoons lemon juice to prevent discoloration. Drain apples. In a large saucepan, combine drained apple slices, lemon slice, sugar, nutmeg, cinnamon, flour and orange juice. Cook over low heat, stirring occasionally.

16. When apples have softened and become golden, remove from heat. Discard lemon slice.

17. Preheat oven to 400F (205C). Pour apple filling into lined pie plate. Arrange pastry strips over top of apples, half in one direction evenly spaced and half across them in the other direction.

18. Brush pastry strips with beaten egg.

19. Roll remaining large piece of pastry to a thickness of 1/4 inch. Cut a circle from the center of the pastry; set aside. Use the ring of pastry left to cover the edges of the pie.

20. Trim excess pastry from edge.

21. Use a small pastry cutter to cut shapes out of remaining pastry circle.

22. Decorate outer rim of pie with pastry shapes. Brush with beaten egg. Score center of each decoration. Bake 40 to 45 minutes. Makes 1 (9-inch) pie.

Apple Turnover

Pastry: 3-1/2 cups all-purpose flour ● 1 teaspoon salt ● 2 tablespoons powdered sugar ● 1/2 cup butter, melted ● 1/4 cup lemon juice ● 2 eggs ● 3 tablespoons milk, if needed **Apple Filling:** 2 lbs. cooking apples, 7 to 8 medium ● 1/3 cup coarsely chopped almonds ● 1/3 cup pine nuts ● 1/3 cup raisins ● 1 teaspoon grated orange peel ● 1 teaspoon ground cinnamon ● 2/3 to 3/4 cup powdered sugar ● 1 cup crumbled cookies, such as Tea Cookies, page 151, or any shortbread cookie ● 2 tablespoons rum or Marsala ● 1/2 cup butter, melted ● 1 to 2 tablespoons apple butter ● 1 egg yolk

1. For pastry, work together flour, salt, sugar, butter, lemon juice and eggs. If necessary, add a few spoonfuls of milk. Wrap dough in plastic wrap. Refrigerate 30 minutes.

2. Preheat oven to 350F (175C). Grease a large baking sheet.

3. For filling, peel and core apples; slice very thinly. Add almonds, pine nuts, raisins, orange peel, cinnamon, sugar, cookie crumbs and rum or Marsala. Blend well.

4. Place 1/2 the dough on a floured pastry cloth or board. Roll out to 1/8 inch thick. Brush with melted butter, then spread with a thin layer of apple butter.

5. Spread 1/2 the filling over 1/2 the rolled dough. Carefully fold other 1/2 of rolled dough over to enclose filling. Seal edges and ends. Use the cloth to roll dough over without tearing it.

6. Still holding the turnover in the cloth, transfer to greased baking sheet. Repeat with remaining dough and filling. Brush surface with egg yolk and melted butter. Bake 40 to 45 minutes or until surface is golden brown. Makes 2 large turnovers.

Chestnut Log

1/2 lb. canned chestnuts ● 2 to 3 tablespoons brandy ● 7 tablespoons butter ● 1 cup sugar ● 3 egg yolks ●
5 tablespoons milk ● 3 cups soft breadcrumbs ● 1/4 teaspoon vanilla extract ● 2 egg whites ●
3 oz. grated semisweet chocolate

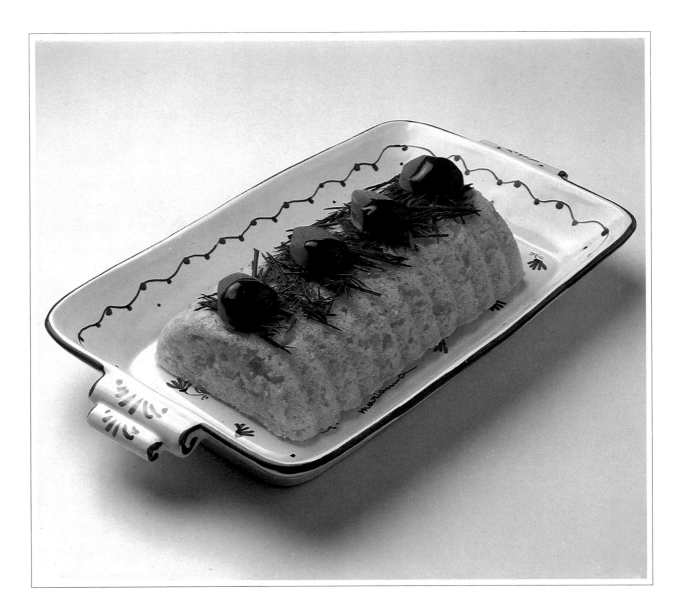

1. Drain chestnuts; reserve 4 chestnuts for decoration. Sprinkle remaining chestnuts with brandy. Allow to stand as long as possible.

2. In a medium bowl, cream together butter and sugar.

3. Lightly beat egg yolks; stir into butter mixture. Gradually stir in milk.

4. Drain chestnuts. Finely chop chestnuts; stir into mixture along with breadcrumbs and vanilla.

5. Beat egg whites until stiff but not dry. Fold carefully into chestnut mixture.

6. Butter an 8-inch Rehrucken mold or an 8-inch loaf pan. Pour mixture into prepared mold or pan; smooth the surface. Cover with buttered foil or waxed paper. Secure with string. Steam gently by placing pan in a baking pan half filled with boiling water. Cover baking pan with foil or lid. Simmer over low heat 40 to 50 minutes.

7. Melt 1 ounce chocolate over low heat. Dip reserved chestnuts in melted chocolate. Let stand until firm.

8. Unmold chestnut log. Decorate with chocolate covered chestnuts and remaining grated chocolate. Makes 1 (8-inch) log.

43

Lemon Meringue Pie

Plain Pastry, page 46   **Lemon Filling:** 1-3/4 cups sugar ● 7 tablespoons cornstarch ● 1/4 teaspoon salt ● 3 eggs, separated ● 1-3/4 cups water ● 1 tablespoon butter or margarine ● 1/2 cup lemon juice ● 1 teaspoon grated lemon peel
Decoration: Peach jelly ● 3 egg whites ● 3/4 cup powdered sugar ● 1/4 cup flaked almonds, toasted

1. For pastry, preheat oven to 400F (205C). Prepare pastry. Roll out pastry; place in an 8- or 9-inch pie plate. Prick pastry with a fork. To prevent pastry from rising during baking, cover with waxed paper weighted with dry beans or peas. Bake 10 to 15 minutes.

2. For filling, in a double boiler or saucepan, combine sugar, cornstarch and salt. Beat egg yolks and water until smooth; stir into sugar mixture. Cook over medium heat until thickened, stirring constantly.

3. Remove from heat. Stir in butter or margarine, lemon juice and lemon peel. Let cool. Beat egg whites until stiff but not dry. Fold carefully into cooled lemon mixture.

4. Pour filling into baked pastry.

5. Melt jelly over low heat. Glaze surface of pie with a thin layer of melted jelly.

6. For meringue topping, beat egg whites until stiff but not dry. Gradually fold in sugar. Using a piping bag fitted with a wavy tip, pipe meringue in diagonal crisscross lines. Decorate edges with a thick band of meringue and flaked almonds. Bake at 400F (205C) 5 minutes to set meringue.

Baked Cheesecake

Plain Pastry: 1 cup all-purpose flour ● 1/2 teaspoon salt ● 1/3 cup unsalted butter ● 3 to 4 tablespoons water
Filling: 1 (8-oz.) and 1 (3-oz.) pkg. cream cheese, room temperature ● 2 eggs ● 3 tablespoons butter, melted ●
1/3 cup all-purpose flour ● 1/2 teaspoon vanilla extract ● 1 teaspoon grated orange peel ● 1/2 cup whipping cream ●
1/4 cup sugar   **Glaze:** 1 egg yolk ● 1/4 cup powdered sugar ● 1/2 tablespoon water

Cheesecake has more or less become the American national dessert. It can be found all over the United States. Its origin however is Roman. In ancient times, the Romans made a tart called *Suavillum,* which was made with pastry, cream cheese and honey. It was eaten throughout the Roman Empire.

TIP: Cheesecake may be served with a fruit topping of your choice.

1. Preheat oven to 400F (205C). In a medium bowl, combine flour and salt. Cut in butter until pieces are size of small peas. Add 3 tablespoons water; toss with a fork until all flour is moistened and mixture begins to form a ball. Add more water to crumbs in bottom of bowl, if necessary. Gather dough into a flat ball. Roll out to a 12-inch circle.

2. Fit pastry into a 10-inch fluted pan, pressing to side and bottom of pan. Do not stretch.

3. Prick lightly with a fork.

4. In a large bowl, beat together cream cheese, eggs and butter.

5. Sift flour gradually into cheese mixture. Blend well. Add vanilla and orange peel.

6. In a separate bowl, whip the cream, gradually adding the sugar.

7. Fold whipped cream carefully into the cheese mixture.

8. Pour cheese mixture into pastry-lined pan; smooth top. To make glaze, combine egg yolk, sugar and water. Glaze top of cheesecake lightly. Bake 20 minutes or until golden brown. Makes 1 (10-inch) cheesecake.

Danish Blueberry & Custard Pastry

Pastry: 1 recipe Brioche Croissant Dough, page 126 ● 1-1/2 cups fresh, frozen or canned blueberries
Custard: 1/4 cup sugar ● 3 tablespoons all-purpose flour ● 2 tablespoons cornstarch ● 1 cup milk ● 2 egg yolks ●
1 tablespoon butter **Glaze:** 2 egg yolks blended with 2 tablespoons water

1. Prepare croissant dough following steps 1 through 7 or until after last folding, rolling and chilling, page 127.

2. For custard, combine sugar, flour and cornstarch. Gradually stir in milk. Cook, stirring constantly, over low heat until mixture thickens and the raw starch taste is gone. This can take up to 30 minutes.

3. Remove from heat. Stir 1/2 cup hot milk mixture into egg yolks. Stir egg-yolk mixture and butter into remaining hot milk mixture. Beat rapidly until blended. Let stand to cool.

4. On a lightly floured surface, roll croissant dough to a 12" x 10" rectangle about 1/3 inch thick. Cut a 4-inch square from the center of one of the long sides. Reserve for lattice top.

5. Grease a large baking sheet. Place dough on baking sheet. Make a depression about 2 inches wide down center of the 3 sides of dough.

6. Spread cooled custard in depression. Cover with blueberries.

7. Roll remaining dough to about half its original thickness. Cut into 1/2-inch strips. Place strips diagonally across filling.

8. Let rise in a warm place 30 to 40 minutes or until doubled in bulk.

9. Preheat oven to 400F (205C). Before baking, brush with egg-yolk glaze. Bake 20 to 25 minutes or until done. Serve warm or cold. Makes 1 large pastry.

TIP: For a sweeter flavor, lightly dust with powdered sugar after baking, or sweeten berries with 2 tablespoons sugar before spreading over custard.

Chestnut Tart

2-1/4 lbs. chestnut flour • 2/3 cup vegetable oil • 1/2 cup plus 1 tablespoon sugar • 1/2 teaspoon salt • 1 cup pine nuts •
1 cup raisins • 1 cup or more water • 1 rosemary sprig

1. Preheat oven to 400F (205C). Lightly oil a 10-inch springform or flan pan.

2. In a large bowl, combine flour, oil, sugar, salt, 3/4 cup pine nuts and 3/4 cup raisins. Add enough water to make a soft batter of pouring consistency.

3. Pour mixture into oiled pan. The paste should not be more than 3/4 to 1 inch thick. If necessary, use a larger pan. Brush surface of paste with oil. Sprinkle with remaining pine nuts, raisins and rosemary.

4. Bake 45 to 55 minutes.

5. To serve, transfer to a serving dish.

Chestnut tart or castagnaccio is a regional dish from the rural part of northern Tuscany. This tart can be served hot or cold, though its subtle flavor is more fully appreciated when it is eaten hot.

Mont Blanc

1 lb. chestnuts (about 4-1/2 cups puree) • 1-1/4 cups milk • 1/2 teaspoon salt • 1 cup sugar • 1 teaspoon vanilla extract •
1/2 cup unsweetened cocoa powder • 2 to 3 tablespoons rum • 2 tablespoons butter or margarine, melted
Decoration: Chantilly Cream, page 195 • Maraschino cherries • Chocolate sprinkles

1. Peel chestnuts as directed on page 34.

2. Cook chestnuts in milk over low heat 45 minutes or until soft. If mixture becomes too dry, add more boiling milk. When soft, drain and press through a ricer or food mill.

3. Add salt, sugar, vanilla, cocoa powder, rum and butter or margarine. Pass mixture through a food mill or ricer again, catching it on a serving plate in a little mound. Refrigerate 1 hour or more.

4. To serve, cover with Chantilly Cream. Decorate with candied cherries and chocolate sprinkles.

TIP: Canned chestnuts may be substituted for fresh ones.

This is a French dessert, originated by the famous Parisian chef, Escoffier.

Christmas Pudding

Pudding: 1 cup shredded suet • 1/2 cup all-purpose flour • 2-1/2 cups fresh white breadcrumbs •
1-1/3 cups raisins • 1-1/3 cups golden raisins • 1 cup currants • 1 cup plus 2 tablespoons packed brown sugar •
1/2 cup chopped blanched almonds • 3/4 cup finely chopped candied fruit • 1/4 teaspoon salt •
1/4 teaspoon ground nutmeg • 1/4 teaspoon ground ginger • 1/4 teaspoon ground cinnamon • 1/4 teaspoon ground mace •
Grated peel and juice of 1/2 lemon • Grated peel and juice of 1/2 orange • 2 tablespoons brandy • 2 tablespoons rum •
1/4 cup brown ale • 2 eggs, beaten • 1/4 cup brandy for flaming
Brandy Butter: 6 tablespoons butter • 1/2 cup sugar • 3 to 4 tablespoons brandy

1. Combine suet, flour, breadcrumbs, raisins, currants, brown sugar, almonds, candied fruit, salt, spices and grated peels in a large bowl. Use your hands to blend thoroughly.

2. In a small bowl, combine lemon juice, orange juice, 2 tablespoons brandy, rum, ale and eggs. Stir into dry ingredients until well blended. Cover and let stand in a cool place overnight.

3. Butter a 3- to 4-cup pudding mold. Stir the mixture; pour into buttered mold. Cover with buttered waxed paper and foil. Secure with string.

4. Place mold in a large saucepan half filled with boiling water. Cover and steam 4 to 4-1/2 hours. Add boiling water, as necessary.

5. Remove pudding; allow to cool. Cover with fresh waxed paper and foil. Store in a cool place until ready to use.

6. For Brandy Butter, cream butter and sugar. Slowly beat in brandy. Refrigerate until firm.

7. To serve, steam pudding 2 hours or until center is firm. Remove foil and waxed paper. Turn pudding out onto a warm serving dish.

8. In a small saucepan, warm 1/4 cup brandy. Pour over pudding. Using a long match, carefully ignite brandy. Serve pudding with Brandy Butter. Makes 1 small pudding.

Cream Wheels with Marrons Glacés

Sponge Cake: 1/4 cup butter • 1/4 cup sugar • 1/3 cup milk • 3/4 cup cake flour • 1 teaspoon vanilla extract • 1 egg •
4 eggs, separated   **Filling:** 1 cup whipping cream • 1 teaspoon vanilla extract • 2 tablespoons powdered sugar •
5 marrons glacés, chopped   **Glaze:** 2 oz. Rum-Sugar Syrup, see Liqueur-Sugar Syrup, page 192

This dessert is known by a variety of names because of its shape.
Technically speaking, the shape is a *vortex*. The cakes are called
wheels, discs and various other names. In the United States, it is
called *jelly roll.*

1. For the cake, preheat oven to 325F (165C). Line a 15" x 10" jelly-roll pan with parchment or waxed paper.

2 In a large saucepan, melt butter and sugar over low heat.

3. Stir in 1/2 the milk. Cook together for a few minutes.

4. Blend in flour and vanilla.

5. Stirring constantly, cook until dough is thick and no longer sticks to pan, 2 to 3 minutes.

6. Remove from heat; cool slightly. Beat in 1 whole egg. Beat in egg yolks, 1 at a time.

7. Add remaining milk, blending well.

8. Pour mixture through a sieve to remove any lumps.

Continued on next page.

9. Cover bowl with plastic wrap; let stand while completing step 10.

10. Beat egg whites until stiff but not dry.

11. Fold carefully into egg mixture.

12. Pour mixture into lined pan; smooth surface. Bake 25 to 30 minutes or until golden brown and tests done.

13. Turn out cake onto a clean cloth. Cool slightly. Remove paper. Roll in cloth. Cool rolled cake completely. In a large bowl, whip the cream. Stir in vanilla and powdered sugar. Unroll cake; trim edges as needed. Spread cream mixture over cake.

14. Sprinkle chopped marrons glacés over cream. Roll cake, taking care that filling does not squeeze out.

15. Wrap roll in waxed paper, taking care that paper touches only the outside of the roll. Let stand in a cool place at least 30 minutes.

16. Remove paper. Brush roll with rum syrup. Cut roll in 1-inch-thick slices. Makes 15 slices.

TIP: If *marrons glacés* or candied chestnuts are not available, substitute 1/4 to 1/2 cup diced strawberries or other fruit.

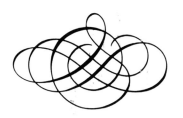

PASTRIES & CREPES

Sicilian Cream Horns

Pastry: 2-1/2 cups all-purpose flour • 1 tablespoon sugar • 1 tablespoon unsweetened cocoa powder • 1 teaspoon finely ground instant coffee • 1/2 teaspoon salt • 1/4 cup butter • 1 egg yolk • 1/2 cup plus 2 tablespoons Marsala • Oil for deep-frying   **Cheese Filling:** 2 cups ricotta or cottage cheese (1 pound) • 1 teaspoon vanilla extract • 2 tablespoons rum • 1/2 cup powdered sugar • 2 oz. chocolate, coarsely grated **Decoration:** 1 cup pistachios, coarsely chopped • 1/2 cup candied lemon peel or orange peel • Candied cherries

1. For pastry, in a medium bowl, combine flour, sugar, cocoa, coffee and salt. Make a well in center of dry ingredients. Add butter, egg yolk and enough Marsala to make a firm but not dry dough. Wrap in plastic wrap or foil. Refrigerate 1 hour.

2. Roll out dough to 1/8 inch thick. Cut into 4-inch squares. Using a rolling pin, round off 2 opposite corners of each square. Lightly moisten non-rounded edges of pastry squares. Place a pastry square around a cannoli tube, joining the non-rounded corners; press to securely seal. Pastries will come off easily if tubes are oiled.

3. In a deep skillet or saucepan, heat oil to 375F (190C) or until a 1-inch cube of bread turns golden brown in 50 seconds. Fry pastries in hot oil 2 to 3 minutes or until golden brown. Remove from oil. Drain well. Cool slightly, then remove metal tube. Cool completely before filling.

4. To make filling, press cheese through a sieve. Beat in vanilla, rum and sugar until smooth. Stir in chocolate. Chill until needed. Use less sugar, if desired.

5. Fill cooled pastries using a spoon or piping bag. Decorate with pistachios, candied peel and cherries as desired. Makes about 18.

Profiteroles

Pastry: 1 cup plus 2 tablespoons water ● 1/2 cup butter ● 1/2 teaspoon salt ● 1 tablespoon sugar ●
1-1/4 cups all-purpose flour ● 3 to 4 eggs, beaten ● 1 teaspoon Marsala for each profiterole, if desired
Cream Filling: 1/2 cup sugar ● 1 tablespoon cornstarch ● 1 tablespoon all-purpose flour ● 1/2 teaspoon vanilla extract ●
1/4 cup milk ● 3 egg yolks, slightly beaten ● 1-1/2 cups whipping cream, whipped
Chocolate Sauce: 5 oz. semisweet chocolate ● 2/3 cup sugar

Profiterole is a French word used to describe the famous dessert
of small choux-pastry balls filled with cream, coated with
chocolate or caramel sauce and piled in a pyramid. It can also be
applied to small savory rolls used to garnish certain soups.

1. For pastry, preheat oven to 400F (205C). In a medium saucepan, combine water, butter, salt and sugar. Place over low heat until butter has melted. Then bring rapidly to a boil. Remove from heat.

2. Beat in flour until it has been absorbed and dough forms a ball. Cool slightly. Add beaten eggs, a little at a time. Each time more beaten egg is added, beat vigorously with a wooden spoon.

3. If the dough is soft enough after the third egg has been added, do not add the fourth. Dough should be shiny and fairly thick.

4. Butter and flour a baking sheet. Using a spoon or a piping bag, place small mounds of dough on baking sheet. Bake 10 minutes; then reduce heat to 350F (175C). Bake 10 to 15 minutes longer.

5. For cream filling, blend sugar, cornstarch, flour and vanilla with milk. Heat until thick. Slowly add this mixture to the egg yolks. Reheat gently, stirring until thickened. Allow to cool.

6. Beat in 1/3 of the whipped cream. Fold in remaining whipped cream. Pour 1 teaspoon Marsala over each profiterole. Using a piping bag and plain tip, fill each profiterole with cream filling. Melt chocolate with sugar. Dip each profiterole in chocolate mixture. Caramel sauce may also be used. Arrange profiteroles in a pyramid on a serving dish. Cover with remaining sauce. Makes about 48.

Brioches with Cream & Fruit

Dough: 1 (1/4-oz) pkg. active dry yeast (1 tablespoon) ● 2 tablespoons warm water (110F, 45C) ● 6 tablespoons warm milk ● 2-1/4 cups all-purpose flour ● 3 eggs ● 1/4 cup sugar ● 1/2 teaspoon salt ● 1/4 cup butter, melted
Decoration: 12 peach or apricot halves ● Chantilly Cream, page 195 ● Liqueur, such as Cointreau, maraschino or kirsch

1. Dissolve yeast in warm water in a small bowl. Add milk and 1/3 cup flour. Cover and let stand in a warm place 15 to 20 minutes or until foamy and doubled in size.

2. Beat eggs. Add remaining flour, yeast mixture, sugar, salt and butter. Knead lightly 5 minutes. Let rise until doubled in bulk, about 1-1/2 hours.

3. Butter and flour individual brioche molds or muffin tins. Fill pans 2/3 full with dough. Cover and let rise a third time until dough has risen to top of molds, about 45 minutes.

4. Preheat oven to 325F (165C). Bake 15 to 20 minutes.

5. Soak brioches in liqueur. To serve, decorate with peach or apricot halves and Chantilly Cream. Makes 12 servings.

The basic recipe for savarins, babas and brioches is the same. They differ only in shape. Babas are made in conical, flat-topped molds, savarin in a ring mold and brioches in smooth-sided brioche molds. The savarin is named after Brillat-Savarin, author of *The Physiology of Taste,* a work containing useful and amusing observations and recipes. This recipe comes from his book and is famous all over the world.

Rum Babas

Brioche Dough, opposite • 1 cup water • 1/2 cup honey • 1/2 cup rum

1. Prepare Brioche Dough.
Bake the dough in baba molds.

2. In a small saucepan,
combine water and honey.
Boil a few minutes. Add rum;
boil 2 to 3 additional minutes.

3. Pierce babas all over with a
skewer to allow syrup to
penetrate. Soak warm babas
in rum syrup. Turn babas
frequently so they absorb as
much syrup as possible. Serve
immediately. Makes 10 to 15
babas.

The rum baba was invented more than two centuries ago by the
cook, who was probably French, to King Stanislas of Poland.
The dough often contains raisins and after baking the babas are
soaked in rum-flavored syrup. Sometimes babas are cooked not
in conical molds but in miniature savarin molds so that their
centers can be decorated with fruit and whipped cream.

Sweet-Potato Pastries

2 lbs. sweet potatoes or yams ● 1 cup butter, room temperature ● 1-1/4 cups all-purpose flour ●
1/4 cup plus 1 tablespoon sugar ● 3 eggs ● 1/4 cup Marsala or other sweet dessert wine ● 1 beaten egg for glaze

1. Cut each sweet potato in half lengthwise. Large potatoes may need to be cut in fourths. Cut out eyes; wash potatoes. Steam until done, 20 to 25 minutes; cool. Carefully remove potato skins, reserving skins.

2. Sieve cooked potatoes or mash with a potato masher until smooth.

3. Preheat oven to 325F (165C). Grease a baking sheet. Melt 1 tablespoon butter in a large saucepan. Stir in sweet potatoes. Add flour and sugar. Stir constantly until blended. Cook, stirring constantly, another 3 to 4 minutes to reduce moisture. Remove from heat.

4. In a small bowl, blend remaining butter with 3 eggs. Add to potato mixture. Return to heat. Beat until blended. Remove from heat. Beat in Marsala or wine.

5. Spread potato mixture generously onto reserved potato skins. Place on greased baking sheet. Extra paste can be baked directly on the greased baking sheet.

6. Brush with beaten egg. Bake 40 to 50 minutes or until golden brown. Makes about 12 pastries.

Cream Doughnuts

Doughnuts: 1 (1/4-oz.) pkg. active dry yeast (1 tablespoon) ● 1/4 cup warm water (110F, 45C) ●
3-1/2 to 4 cups all-purpose flour ● 1/2 cup milk ● 6 tablespoons butter or margarine ● 3 eggs ● 3 tablespoons rum ●
1/3 cup sugar ● 1/2 teaspoon salt ● 1 teaspoon vanilla extract ● Oil for deep-frying   **Filling:** Pastry Cream, page 194
Decoration: Powdered sugar

1. Dissolve yeast in warm water. Combine 1/2 cup flour, 1/4 cup milk and yeast mixture. Let stand 15 to 20 minutes or until foamy.

2. Melt butter or margarine; cool. Add eggs and rum. Stir in 3 cups flour, sugar, salt, vanilla, remaining 1/4 cup milk and yeast mixture. If necessary, add a little more flour to make a soft, smooth dough.

3. Cover and let rise in a warm place until doubled in bulk, about 1 hour.

4. Turn out dough on a lightly floured surface. Knead 10 minutes or until it no longer sticks to your fingers. Roll out dough until 1/4 to 1/2 inch thick. Using a 3-inch round cutter, cut circles from dough. Sprinkle circles lightly with flour. Cover and let rise 30 minutes or until doubled in bulk.

5. In a deep skillet or saucepan, heat oil to 375F (190C) or until a 1-inch cube of bread turns golden brown in 50 seconds. Fry doughnuts until golden brown, about 5 minutes. Drain well.

6. Fill doughnuts with Pastry Cream using a piping bag.

7. Before serving, sprinkle with powdered sugar. Makes 20 to 24 doughnuts.

Petits Fours

Almond Sponge: 9 egg yolks ● 1/2 cup sugar ● 1/2 teaspoon almond extract ● 7 egg whites ● 1-1/4 cups all-purpose flour ● 1 cup finely ground almonds   **Filling:** 1 cup Apricot-Jam Glaze, see Jam Glaze, page 196 ● 1 lb. Almond Paste, page 193
Icing: 3/4 lb. Fondant Icing, page 195   **Decoration:** Candied fruits, pistachios or marzipan shapes

1. Preheat oven to 400F (205C). Line a 15" x 10" baking pan with waxed paper. Oil paper on both sides.

2. For cake, beat egg yolks and sugar over hot water until mixture is nearly white in color and ribbons form when beater is lifted, 5 to 8 minutes with an electric mixer. Remove from heat. Stir in almond extract.

3. Beat egg whites until stiff but not dry. Fold 1/4 of beaten egg whites into egg-yolk mixture. Combine flour and ground almonds. Sift 1/2 the flour and almond mixture over batter; fold in. Fold in 1/2 the remaining egg whites and all of remaining flour mixture. Carefully fold in remaining egg whites. Pour batter into lined pan. Bake 15 to 20 minutes.

4. Remove from oven. Turn out cake onto a wire rack; peel off paper. Cut off any hard or dark edges. Cut cake in half crosswise.

5. Brush surface of both halves with Apricot-Jam Glaze.

6. Roll out almond paste between 2 pieces of oiled waxed paper until same size as a cake half.

7. Sandwich cake halves together, placing almond paste between glazed surfaces.

8. Cut sandwiched cake into small shapes; brush each with Apricot-Jam Glaze. Cover with Fondant Icing, tinted any desired color.

9. Before icing firms, decorate with candied fruit, pistachios, marzipan shapes or as desired. Makes about 18.

Orange or Raisin Crepes

Crepe batter: 3 egg yolks • 2/3 cup milk • 2/3 cup half and half • 6 tablespoons orange liqueur • 1 cup all-purpose flour •
1/4 cup sugar • 1/4 teaspoon salt • 1 egg white • 3 tablespoons butter or margarine   **Orange Filling:**
1/4 cup butter or margarine • 1/2 cup sugar • 1 teaspoon grated orange peel • 1/3 cup cognac • 2/3 cup orange juice •
Orange slices   **Raisin Filling:** 3/4 cup raisins • 1/2 cup rum or brandy • 1/4 cup butter or margarine • 1/2 cup sugar

Crepes are thin, crisp pancakes that brown in a lacy pattern as they cook. The name comes from the Latin *crispus,* meaning crisp. Crepes can be served as a sweet or savory dish. For savory pancakes, the batter is made in the same way, but without the cream, sugar or liqueur. This basic recipe may be adapted and any number of different kinds of filling substituted.

In crepes containing grated orange peel, an orange liqueur should be used. In crepes containing only orange juice, use cognac or brandy. In crepes containing raisins, use rum, cognac or brandy.

1. Beat egg yolks; add milk, half and half, and orange liqueur. Sift flour, sugar and salt into mixture; blend well. There should be no lumps.

2. Beat egg white until stiff but not dry; fold into batter.

3. Cover and let stand 10 to 15 minutes.

4. Melt butter or margarine; add to batter.

5. Over medium heat, warm a medium skillet that has been greased with butter or margarine. When pan starts to smoke, pour in enough batter to thinly cover base of pan. Shake pan to prevent crepe from sticking.

6. When bottom is golden, turn crepe to cook other side. Repeat with remaining batter.

7. For orange crepes, beat together butter or margarine, sugar, orange peel and cognac. Stir in orange juice. Cook over low heat, stirring until thickened. Spread each crepe with a spoonful of this sauce. Roll and arrange on a serving dish. Pour remaining sauce over crepes. Decorate with orange slices.

8. For raisin crepes, chop raisins. Soak chopped raisins in rum or brandy. Melt butter or margarine and sugar together in a saucepan. Add soaked raisins and any remaining liqueur. Cook over low heat, stirring until thickened. Spread each crepe with a spoonful of this sauce. Roll and arrange on a serving dish. Pour remaining sauce over crepes. Serve immediately. Makes 16 to 18 crepes.

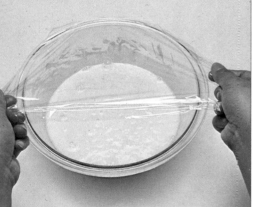

Crepes Suzette

Crepe batter, page 66   **Orange Sauce:** 1/4 cup butter or margarine ● 1/2 cup sugar ● 3/4 cup orange juice ●
1/4 cup lemon juice ● 1 teaspoon grated orange peel ● 1 teaspoon grated lemon peel ● 1/2 cup orange liqueur ●
1/4 cup cognac for flaming

1. Prepare crepe batter following method on page 67.

2. For sauce, melt butter or margarine in a skillet over low heat. Stir in sugar, orange and lemon juice, and orange and lemon peel. Allow liquid to evaporate slightly so sauce thickens, then stir in liqueur.

3. Cook crepes, page 67. Immerse each crepe in Orange Sauce. Fold crepe in quarters; arrange on a serving dish.

4. To flame, warm the cognac. Sprinkle lightly over crepes. Carefully ignite. Serve immediately. Makes 16 to 18 crepes.

Tradition has it that crepes were first given the name Suzette by Edward VII of England. The King was taken with the beauty of one of his guests named Suzette, just at the moment when, by mistake, his French chef Henri Carpenter had allowed the liqueur in the pan to ignite. As if nothing were amiss, the chef served the flaming pancakes.

The following variations of the basic crepe recipe are suggested: Lemon Crepes, with lemon juice and sugar; Chocolate Crepes, with melted chocolate; Ice-Cream Crepes, with vanilla ice cream, orange juice, sugar and Calvados; Crepes a L'Imperiale, with red-currant jelly, crumbled macaroons and pineapple; Crepes Flambés au Grand Marnier; and Crepes Irene, with blackberries, vanilla ice cream, honey, hazelnuts and brandy.

Bulgarian Apples

For each serving: 1 Sweet-Shortcrust-Pastry tart base, page 196 ● 1 large cooking apple ● 1/3 cup water ●
1 cup red wine ● 1 tablespoon sugar ● 1 tablespoon yogurt ● 3 tablespoons Cream Custard, page 194
Filling, if desired: 1 to 2 tablespoons currant jelly mixed with 1 tablespoon chopped nuts

1. Prepare tart base. Peel and core apple.

2. In a medium saucepan, combine water, wine and sugar. Add apple; cook until tender.

3. Combine yogurt and Cream Custard. Pipe a layer about 1/2 inch thick on tart base.

4. Place apple on top.

5. If desired, fill apple with jelly-nut mixture.

There are hundreds of different ways to cook apples. They are often baked in the oven and are usually cooked with sugar and occasionally with wine or a liqueur, such as Calvados. Among the best known recipes are: Apples Frederic, with lemon cream, sponge cake and maraschino liqueur; Apples Josephine, a French recipe using rice and raspberry syrup; Apples Parisiennes, with various fruit in syrup, chopped almonds and Calvados; Spanish Apples, with fruit in syrup, chopped almonds, dried figs, candied cherries and honey; Baked Apples with blueberries; Apples Cardinal, with vanilla cream, fruit in syrup, hazelnuts, orange juice, curacao and topped with red cherries to resemble a cardinal's hat, hence the name.

Cream Puffs

Choux Paste: 1-1/8 cups water ● 1/2 cup butter ● 1 tablespoon sugar ● 1-1/4 cups all-purpose flour ●
1/2 teaspoon vanilla extract or 1 teaspoon grated lemon peel ● 3 to 4 eggs
Filling: Chantilly Cream, page 195, or Pastry Cream, page 194

Choux Paste is used for profiteroles and chocolate eclairs. It can
also be used for savory dishes, in which case salt, spice or cheese
are used instead of sugar. The filling can be mixed with fresh or
candied fruit.

1. For Choux Paste, preheat oven to 400F (205C). In a large saucepan, bring water, butter and sugar to a boil over medium heat. Remove from heat as soon as mixture begins to boil.

2. Sift flour into mixture.

3. Return to heat; stir vigorously with a wooden spoon until mixture thickens and comes away from the side of the pan. Reduce heat to low. Continue stirring 2 to 3 minutes. Remove from heat. Cool slightly.

4. Add vanilla or lemon peel. Add eggs, 1 at a time, beating until smooth before next addition.

5. Paste should not be too soft. If it is, the liquid was not reduced enough in step 3. To avoid too soft a mixture, do not add the fourth egg unless necessary.

6. Grease and flour a baking sheet.

7. Spoon the paste in small heaps on prepared baking sheet with a teaspoon or force through a piping bag. Bake 25 to 30 minutes or until lightly browned and firm to touch. Allow to cool.

8. For filling, prepare Chantilly Cream or Pastry Cream. Fill cream puffs. Makes 16 (3-inch) cream puffs.

Fruit Tarts

Sweet Shortcrust Pastry: 5 tablespoons butter or margarine ● 1/2 cup sugar ● 1 egg ● 1 teaspoon vanilla extract ●
1-1/4 cups all-purpose flour   **Custard & Fruit Filling:** About 1/2 cup apricot jam ● About 1 cup Cream Custard or
Confectioner's Custard, page 194 ● Fresh or canned fruit   **Almond-Cream Filling:** 1/2 cup butter, room temperature ●
3/4 cup powdered sugar ● 3 egg yolks, slightly beaten ● 2 tablespoons rum ● Scant 1 cup ground almonds
Glaze: Kirsch Syrup, see Liqueur-Sugar Syrup, page 192 ● Apricot jelly

1. For pastry, in a medium
bowl, stir butter or margarine
until creamy.

2. Gradually beat in sugar.

3. Stir in egg and vanilla.

4. Stir in flour; blend until
pastry forms a smooth ball.

5. Cover and let stand 20 to 30
minutes.

6. On a lightly floured surface,
knead dough 1 minute.

Continued on next page.

These fruit tarts are well known and popular the world over.
This recipe is the classic method of preparation, which, though
elegant, is not complicated. The tarts can be cut into a variety of
shapes and can be made smaller or larger, with a sweet
shortcrust base and a fruit filling and glaze of your choice.

7. Flatten dough with palm of your hand.

8. Roll out dough.

9. Shape dough into a rectangle.

10. Continue rolling until 1/8 inch thick.

11. Cut out 4-inch circles.

12. Fit pastry circles into tart pans, pressing firmly against sides. Do not stretch.

13. Trim extra pastry from edge of tart pans.

14. Spoon 1/4 teaspoon jam into each pastry-lined tart pan; set aside. Preheat oven to 350F (175C).

15. For Almond-Cream Filling, in a medium bowl, beat 1/2 cup butter until creamy. Gradually beat in powdered sugar, egg yolks and rum.

16. Stir in ground almonds. Spoon almond mixture into a pastry bag.

17. Pipe almond mixture into each tart, filling evenly. Bake 15 minutes. Cool on a rack; remove tarts from pans.

18. To glaze, generously brush each baked tart with syrup. Filling will absorb syrup.

19. In a small saucepan, melt jelly; brush over each tart.

20. Using a pastry bag with round tip, pipe about 1 tablespoon custard into each tart.

21. Soak fruit of choice in remaining syrup.

22. Place soaked fruit on each tart. Makes about 12 tarts.

Nuns' Chatter

2-1/2 cups all-purpose flour ● 3/4 cup granulated sugar ● 1/2 teaspoon salt ● 1/4 cup butter, room temperature ●
1 teaspoon grated lemon peel or orange peel ● 1 teaspoon vanilla extract ● 1 egg ● 2 egg yolks ●
1/4 cup Marsala or other liqueur ● 2 tablespoons orange juice ● Milk, if needed ● Oil for deep-frying ●
Powdered sugar

1. Combine flour, 3/4 cup sugar and salt. Beat in butter. Add lemon or orange peel. Add vanilla, egg, egg yolks, liqueur and orange juice. Stir in a few spoonfuls of milk, if necessary. Dough should be firm enough to roll out thinly with a rolling pin.

2. Knead dough lightly. Roll out to 1/8 inch thick. Using a pastry wheel, cut ribbons not wider than 1-1/2 to 2 inches by 3 to 4 inches long. Cut 2 lengthwise slits in the middle of each ribbon. Twist each ribbon carefully.

3. In a deep skillet, bring oil to 375F (190C) or until a 1-inch cube of bread turns golden brown in 50 seconds. Fry pastry, a few at at a time, until lightly browned.

4. Drain well. Roll in powdered sugar. Makes 55 to 60 cookies.

The Italian name for these fried sweets, and perhaps their original name, is *nuns' ribbons*. This name is now lost in a mass of regional names. In Lombardy, the ribbons have become *chiacchiere* which means chatter. This is now the most frequently used name, more common than any of the other regional terms. Chiacchiere is a carnival sweet made all over Italy, often with slight variations.

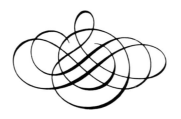

FRUIT DESSERTS

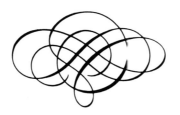

Glazed Fresh Fruit

Glacé Icing or Liqueur-Flavored Glacé Icing, page 195 ● Fresh fruit of choice

1. Prepare Glacé Icing.

2. Wash fruit; pat dry with paper towels.

3. Dip fruit into icing; let harden.

4. One pound of fruit will serve 3 to 4 people.

Peaches in Kirsch

Cake: 1/4 cup butter or margarine ● 1-1/3 cups cake flour ● 4 eggs ● 1 cup powdered sugar ● 1 teaspoon vanilla extract ●
2 tablespoons kirsch or Cointreau **Frangipane Cream:** 2 egg yolks ● 1/2 cup sugar ● 1/4 cup all-purpose flour ●
1/4 cup ground toasted almonds ● 1 cup milk ● 1 teaspoon vanilla extract **Cream Edging:** 1-3/4 cups powdered sugar ●
2 tablespoons kirsch or Cointreau ● 4 egg whites ● 1/2 cup ground almonds ● Chantilly Cream, page 195
Decoration: 20 fresh or canned peach slices ● 2 to 3 tablespoons Caramelized Sugar, page 192

1. This cake is usually baked in a paper case about 12" x 4-1/2" x 1-1/4 ". Case can also be made from foil. Grease and flour case. Preheat oven to 325F (170C).

2. Melt butter or margarine; cool slightly.

3. Sift flour.

4. In a medium bowl over hot water, beat together eggs and sugar.

5. Remove from heat; beat vigorously.

6 Continue to beat until mixture is thick and light in color.

Continued on next page.

7. Fold in flour; stir in vanilla.

8. Stir in cooled butter or margarine.

9. Pour mixture into paper or foil case. Bake 35 to 40 minutes or until cake tests done.

10. The cake is done when a wooden pick inserted in center comes out clean. Remove cake from oven.

11. Turn cake upside-down; allow to cool.

12. For Frangipane Cream, beat together egg yolks and sugar until mixture is pale and smooth.

13. Fold in flour and almonds.

14. Stir in milk and vanilla.

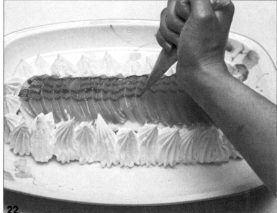

15. Pour mixture through a sieve to remove lumps.

16. Stir mixture constantly over low heat until smooth and thick, 8 to 10 minutes.

17. For cream edging, melt powdered sugar in kirsch or Cointreau over low heat; remove from heat.

18. Beat egg whites; beat in melted sugar. Fold in almonds and Chantilly Cream.

19. To assemble cake, generously brush cake with kirsch or Cointreau.

20. Spread a layer of Frangipane Cream about 1/2 inch thick over entire cake.

21. Arrange peach slices on top of Frangipane Cream. Using a piping bag, pipe cream edging around fruit.

22. Decorate peaches with Caramelized Sugar using a piping bag and a very fine tip. Just before serving, sprinkle more kirsch or Cointreau over peaches.

Stuffed Fruit & Nuts

Almond Paste, page 193 ● Food coloring, if desired ● Dried dates, prunes, apricots, peaches or other dried fruit ●
Halved walnuts, pecans, almonds or other nuts

1. Prepare Almond Paste.
Add food coloring of choice,
if desired.

2. Cut dried fruit in halves or
leave attached at one side.
Remove stones.

3. Shape almond paste in balls
about the size of walnuts.
Press into fruit halves or
sandwich between 2 nut
halves.

4. Each piece of fruit or
sandwiched nut makes 1
appetizer serving.

Variation

Dip stuffed fruit and nuts into
melted semisweet chocolate;
let harden.

Baked Apple

For each serving: 1 large baking apple ● 1 tablespoon apricot jam or peach jam ● 1 shortbread cookie or macaroon, crumbled ●
1 teaspoon butter ● Sliced almonds ● 1 teaspoon sugar ● 1/3 cup Marsala or port wine

1. Preheat oven to 350F (175C). Butter a baking dish large enough for the number of apples prepared.

2. Wash and dry apple. Remove core. With a sharp knife, cut a circle around apple, 1 inch from top. Place cored apple in buttered baking dish.

3. In a small bowl, combine jam and cookie crumbs. Spoon into center of apple.

4. Dot filled apple with butter and sliced almonds.

5. Sprinkle with sugar. Sugar will form a crust while apple bakes.

6. Pour wine into baking dish. Bake apple 30 minutes or until tender. Serve hot or cold. Each apple makes 1 serving.

Pears in White Wine

3 large pears • 1/2 cup sugar • About 2/3 cup white wine • About 2/3 cup water • Strip of lemon peel • 2 whole cloves

1. Peel pears; cut in halves and remove cores.

2. Place peeled, cored pears in a large saucepan. Reserve 1/3 cup wine. Add remaining ingredients to saucepan.

3. Simmer over medium-low heat until pears are tender, about 10 minutes.

4. Use a slotted spoon to place pears in a serving bowl.

5. Add reserved wine to cooking liquid. Bring to a boil. Reduce heat; simmer 5 to 10 minutes until liquid is slightly reduced.

6. Remove and discard cloves and lemon peel. Pour syrup over pears; cool before serving. Makes 2 to 3 servings.

Fruit Salad

2 lbs. fresh or 2 (1-lb.) cans apples, pears, strawberries, oranges, peaches, apricots, cherries, pineapple, raspberries or other fruit •
1 cup chopped walnuts • 1/2 cup sugar • 1/8 teaspoon vanilla extract • Juice of 1 lemon •
2 to 3 tablespoons rum or maraschino liqueur • 2-1/4 cups half and half • 1/2 cup coarsely chopped dried fruit •
1/4 cup pine nuts

1. Wash, drain and peel fresh fruit, if necessary. Slice fresh or canned fruit.

2. In a large bowl, combine sliced fruits and 1 cup chopped nuts.

3. In a medium bowl, combine sugar, vanilla, lemon juice and rum or liqueur. Pour over fruit and nuts; stir gently.

4. Add half and half. Sprinkle dried fruit and pine nuts over top.

5. Refrigerate 2 to 3 hours before serving. Makes 6 to 8 servings.

Turkish Oranges

6 oranges • Water • 1-3/4 cups sugar • 2 whole cloves

1. Peel oranges, removing only colored peel. Do not include white pith. Cut peel into thin strips.

2. In a medium saucepan, cover peel with cold water. Bring to a boil. Cook until tender; drain.

3. In a large heavy skillet, combine sugar, 1/3 cup water and cloves. Stir over medium heat until sugar dissolves. Reduce heat; simmer until mixture begins to caramelize, stirring occasionally. Remove cloves.

4. Add cooked shredded peel and about 1/3 cup water. Stir until peel is coated with syrup. Set aside to cool.

5. Use a sharp knife to cut pith and membrane from outside of each orange. Arrange peeled oranges on a serving dish. Spoon syrup and caramelized peel over oranges, turning oranges to cover evenly.

6. Refrigerate 2 to 3 hours. Before serving, quarter oranges from top to bottom. Makes 6 servings.

Peach Melba

2 pints fresh raspberries or 1 (8-oz.) jar seedless raspberry jam • 2 to 4 tablespoons warm water • 1 cup powdered sugar •
1/4 cup lemon juice • 1/8 teaspoon vanilla extract • 2 to 3 tablespoons raspberry liqueur or other sweet liqueur •
6 fresh peaches, peeled, halved or 12 canned peach halves • 1 cup granulated sugar • 2 cups water • 1 quart vanilla ice cream

1. Rinse fresh raspberries. Puree raspberries and 1/4 cup water in a blender or food processor; sieve to remove seeds. If using jam, heat in saucepan with about 2 tablespoons water.

2. In a large bowl, combine raspberry puree or heated jam mixture, powdered sugar, lemon juice, vanilla and liqueur. Refrigerate 1 hour.

3. To prepare fresh peaches, in a large saucepan, combine granulated sugar and 2 cups water. Stir over medium heat until sugar dissolves. Add fresh peach halves. Poach 5 to 10 minutes until just tender. Cool peaches in syrup.

4. Place a shallow layer of ice cream in bottoms of 6 glasses or dessert dishes. Top each with 2 cooked or canned peach halves, then 2 scoops of ice cream. Pour raspberry mixture over each.

5. Serve immediately. Makes 6 servings.

This recipe was created nearly a century ago by the celebrated French chef, Auguste Escoffier, in honor of Dame Nellie Melba, the famous Australian soprano. The most important gastronomic innovations of the last century, it seems, have been linked to the world of opera, either to singers like Melba or to composers like Rossini and Bellini.

Hawaiian Fruit Salad

1 large fresh pineapple ● 2 bananas ● Juice of 1/2 lemon ● 2 kiwifruit ● 1 mango ● 3 or 4 lettuce leaves ●
1 orange or tangerine, peeled, segmented ● 10 maraschino cherries, drained ● 2 tablespoons sugar
Orange Cream: 1/2 cup orange juice ● 1/4 cup sugar ● 1 egg yolk, beaten ● 3/4 cup whipping cream

Fruit salads are often served with half and half, whipping cream
or sweet liqueur, such as Marsala, maraschino or kirsch. This
one has an unusual cream dressing. Some more elaborate fruit
salads are garnished with yogurt, cream cheese, chopped toasted
nuts or whole nuts, such as pine nuts.

1. Wash pineapple before cutting in half. Ripe pineapple should give slightly when pressed with your fingers. Cut pineapple in half. Reserve 1/2 of pineapple for another use.

2. Remove hard core from center of other pineapple half. Use a sharp knife to cut fruit from shell. Cut around outside, then slice lengthwise and crosswise for easy removal of fruit with a spoon.

3. Lay empty pineapple half, cut-side down, on a cloth to drain.

4. Peel and slice bananas; sprinkle with lemon juice to prevent browning.

5. Peel and slice kiwifruit.

6. Peel mango; remove stone and cut fruit into pieces.

7. Arrange lettuce leaves in drained pineapple half. Add pineapple pieces, sliced bananas, kiwifruit and mango pieces, orange or tangerine segments and cherries. Sprinkle with 2 tablespoons sugar; set aside.

8. For Orange Cream, in a small saucepan, combine orange juice and 1/4 cup sugar. Stir over low heat until sugar dissolves. Gradually whisk in egg yolk. Stir over low heat until mixture thickens. Cool completely. Whip cream until slightly thickened; fold into orange mixture. Pour over salad at serving time. Makes 4 to 6 servings.

Melon Portuguese-Style

1 (2-lb.) cantaloupe or honeydew melon ● 1/4 cup sugar ● 1/2 teaspoon ground cinnamon ● 1 cup white port ●
Chantilly Cream, page 195

1. With stem-end up, cut off top of melon in a zig-zag pattern. Scoop out seeds.

2. Use a melon baller to remove fruit from shell.

3. Replace melon balls in shell. Stir in sugar and cinnamon; let stand 15 minutes.

4. Add port; refrigerate 1 hour.

5. Serve in small glasses, topped with dollops of Chantilly Cream.

This fruit salad is served in the melon shell. It can be prepared in various ways. Add blueberries and a sprinkling of pistachios, use kirsch or maraschino liqueur instead of port wine, or add other mixed fruits to melon. Top with vanilla ice cream and brandy. Or add pineapple, bananas and kirsch.

EXOTIC DESSERTS

Manjyu

Filling: 1-1/4 cups red azuki beans ● 3/4 cup sugar ● 1/2 teaspoon salt
Covering: 1/3 cup grated Japanese yam or yellow sweet potato ● 3/4 cup rice flour ● 1/2 cup sugar ● 1 to 2 teaspoons water
Decoration: Few drops sour cherry syrup

1. Soak beans 1 hour in cold water to cover. Boil beans in water to cover over medium heat 45 to 60 minutes or until tender. Add water, if necessary. Skim surface frequently until surface is clear.

2. Drain beans; return to pan over low heat. Add sugar. Stir until sugar dissolves and moisture disappears.

3. Remove from heat; stir in salt. Allow to cool.

4. Form cooled mixture into 20 small balls. Coat your hands lightly with rice flour so the mixture does not stick.

5. Reduce grated yam to a pulp using a mortar and pestle. Stir in rice flour and sugar, adding a little water if necessary. Do not make too moist. Dough becomes more moist as it stands.

6. Form mixture into 20 balls. Flatten balls into circles between the palms of your hands.

7. Place a ball of the bean filling in the center of each circle. Enclose the ball in the circle.

8. Place a damp cloth in the bottom of a steamer. Arrange bean balls, seam-side down, on the cloth.

9. Steam rapidly for 8 minutes.

10. Cool the sweets using a fan. The more air fanned over the sweets, the glossier the surface of the sweets will be.

11. Before serving, pour a drop of sour cherry syrup on each sweet. Makes 20 servings.

Japanese Oranges

3/4 cup red azuki beans • 1-1/3 cups sugar • 1/2 teaspoon salt • 1 cup rice • 2 cups water • 2 tablespoons soya flour •
2 tablespoons sugar • Pinch of salt • 1/4 cup toasted sesame seeds, coarsely chopped • 2 tablespoons sugar • Pinch of salt

1. Soak beans 1 hour in cold water to cover. Boil beans in water to cover over medium heat 45 to 60 minutes or until slightly tender. Do not overcook. Add water, if necessary.

2. Skim surface frequently until surface is clear.

3. Drain beans; return to pan over low heat. Add sugar. Cook, stirring carefully, until reduced, about 20 minutes. Stir in salt.

4. Transfer to a large dish; allow to cool.

5. Boil rice in 2 cups salted water 12 to 15 minutes or until tender. Drain well; allow to stand a few minutes. Then pound with a wooden pestle or the end of a rolling pin.

6. Form 20 small balls with the pounded rice. Divide azuki paste into 20 portions. Spread a damp cloth over the palm of your left hand, place a portion of azuki paste on the cloth and flatten slightly. Place a ball of rice in the middle then wrap the cloth round both with your hand and squeeze into a ball. Repeat until all 20 balls are covered.

7. In a small bowl, combine soya flour, 2 tablespoons sugar, and a pinch of salt. In another small bowl, combine sesame seeds, 2 tablespoons sugar and pinch of salt.

8. Roll 1/3 the balls in soya mixture, 1/3 the balls in sesame seed mixture and leave 1/3 the balls plain. Makes 20 servings.

In ancient times this dessert was known by two different names depending on the season of the year. In spring it was called *botamochi*, from the Japanese name for the peony. In autumn it was called *ohaghi*, from a plant called *haghi*. Today it is traditionally eaten during higan, a Buddhist religious festival.

Sweet-Potato Balls

1 medium or large yellow sweet potato ● 1/3 cup granulated or 1/2 cup powdered sugar ● 1/4 teaspoon salt ●
1 teaspoon green tea powder or 1 to 2 drops green food coloring ● 4 chestnuts, cooked, peeled, or 4 marrons glacés

These Japanese sweets can be molded in various ways. You can
make them whichever shape you prefer. Cook fresh chestnuts or
use marrons glacés. Then cut each chestnut or marron glacé into
halves.

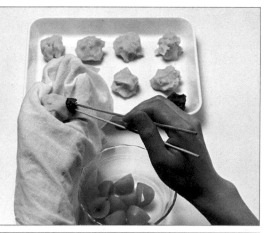

1. Wash, peel and cut sweet potato into 1/2-inch slices. Soak slices in water 30 minutes so that they lose their bitter flavor.

2. Cover slices with water; boil until tender.

3. Drain well; sieve cooked potato slices while still warm. Use a wooden spatula to press them through a sieve.

4. Place potato pulp in a saucepan. Add sugar; bring to a boil, stirring constantly. Stir in salt. Remove from heat. Allow to cool.

5. Make 9 equal balls. Mix 1 ball with the tea powder or 1 to 2 drops green food color. Spread a damp cloth over the palm of your left hand. Place 1 of the 8 balls in your hand. Add 1/8 of the green ball.

6. Flatten the ball, using the edge of the cloth, and form a flat 4-inch circle. The green part should be on the outside of the circle.

7. Place half a chestnut in the center of each circle.

8. Using the cloth, close the circle around the chestnut. Shape into a firm ball. Repeat steps 5 to 8 for the remaining balls of paste.

Misuyokan

1-3/4 cups red azuki beans ● 1-3/4 cups sugar ● 1/2 teaspoon salt ●
1 stick tengusa gelatin or 2 (1/4-oz.) pkgs. unflavored gelatin ● 2 cups water

This is a typical Japanese summer sweet. Tengusa is a kind of
seaweed. The gelatin obtained from it is called *kanten* and can be
found in Oriental-food specialty stores.

1. Cook azuki beans as directed on page 95, step 1. Drain beans; mash beans through a sieve with a wooden pestle. Discard skins left in the sieve. Or, puree beans in a food processor.

2. Place pureed beans in a muslin cloth; squeeze hard to remove excess water. The bean paste remains in the cloth.

3. Place bean paste in a saucepan over very low heat. Stir in 1-1/2 cups sugar until paste has thickened; then stir in salt.

4. If using tengusa gelatin, soak in water 30 minutes. Wrap it in a cloth and squeeze. Dissolve completely in 2 cups water in a pan over medium heat. Add remaining sugar; stir to dissolve.

5. Remove from heat and strain through a cloth placed over a metal sieve. If using granular gelatin, soften gelatin 5 minutes in 2 cups cold water. Place over low heat until dissolved. Stir in remaining 1/4 cup sugar until dissolved.

6. Return gelatin to heat; gradually add bean paste, stirring constantly. When mixture begins to boil, reduce heat and cook 2 to 3 minutes. Season to taste with salt.

7. Remove from heat. Cool quickly by placing pan in cold water; stir constantly.

8. Lightly moisten an 8-inch-square pan. Turn cooled mixture into dampened pan. Allow to set in a cool place. Turn out and cut into blocks.

Dango—Sweets for the Mitarashi Festival

Dough: 1-1/2 cups rice flour • 1/2 cup plus 2 tablespoons warm water   **Sauce:** 3 tablespoons sugar • 3 tablespoons water • 3 tablespoons soy sauce • 1 tablespoon cornstarch

1. Make a dough with the rice flour and 1/2 cup warm water. Add a little more water, if necessary, to make a dough that sticks together.

2. Spread a damp cloth over the base of a steamer. Break the dough roughly into large pieces by hand and place on the cloth. Steam over fast boiling water 20 to 30 minutes.

3. As soon as the pieces are cooked, pound with a wooden pestle until mixture becomes one mass. Divide resulting paste in half. Roll each piece into a long roll, 3/4 inch in diameter.

4. Place in ice water a few minutes to harden; dry with a cloth. Cut into 3/4-inch pieces. Roll each piece by hand into a ball.

5. Wet wooden skewers and thread 4 to 5 balls onto each skewer.

6. Combine sauce ingredients in a small saucepan. Cook over low heat, stirring until thickened.

7. Broil or grill dough balls until they begin to turn dark brown.

8. Place the balls on a serving dish; cover with sauce. Makes about 12 balls.

Warabi Mochi

1/2 cup rice flour • 1 cup warabi flour • 1-3/4 cups powdered sugar • 1-1/4 cups water • Soya-bean flour •
Granulated sugar to taste

1. In a large saucepan, combine rice flour, warabi flour and powdered sugar. Gradually stir in water.

2. Stir constantly over medium heat until mixture is transparent.

3. Pour into an 8-inch-square pan. Let cool, then refrigerate until set.

4. Turn out of pan; cut into squares.

5. Combine a little soya flour and granulated sugar. Sprinkle over cubes before serving. Makes about 6 servings.

Warabi is a Japanese term for the plant *pteridium aquilinium,* a kind of fern. Warabi flour is sometimes available from Oriental-food specialty stores. *Mochi* is the name of a type of rice. This is a summer dessert, fresh and attractive.

Candied Sweet Potatoes

2 medium sweet potatoes ● 2 cups sugar ● 2/3 cup water ● Sugar crystals

1. Wash sweet potatoes. Do not peel potatoes. Cut into 1/2-inch thick slices. Soak potato slices in water about 1 hour.

2. Boil potatoes 8 to 10 minutes, but do not allow them to become too soft. Rinse in cold water. Drain well and cool.

3. Melt 1-1/2 cups sugar in a saucepan with 2/3 cup water.

4. Add cooked potato slices. Remove from heat as soon as mixture boils. Let stand 5 hours.

5. Return to heat and remove again just as boiling point is reached.

6. Remove potatoes from this syrup. Add 1/4 cup sugar to syrup. Stir over low heat until sugar is dissolved. Add potatoes. Cook again, removing from heat as soon as boiling point is reached. Let stand 3 hours.

7. Repeat step 6 adding the last 1/4 cup sugar and letting the potatoes stand 1 hour.

8. Cool completely, then drain. Roll potato slices in sugar crystals. Makes about 20 slices.

Wheel of Happiness—Watermelon & Lychees with Lemon Jelly

1 (1/4-oz.) pkg. unflavored gelatin • 1/2 cup cold water • 1 cup hot water • 3/4 cup granulated or 1 cup powdered sugar • 1/4 cup lemon juice • 1 small watermelon • 1 small can lychees

1. In a small saucepan, soak gelatin in cold water 5 minutes to soften. Add hot water; stir constantly over low heat until completely dissolved.

2. Stir in sugar until completely dissolved. Remove from heat; stir in lemon juice.

3. Rinse an 8-inch ring mold with cold water. Fill with hot gelatin mixture. Refrigerate until firmly set.

4. Remove seeds from watermelon. Scoop out flesh with a melon-baller. Drain lychees. If using fresh lychees, remove skin and stones.

5. To serve, unmold gelatin onto a serving dish. Surround with fruit balls. Makes 4 to 6 servings.

Sesame-Seed Balls

1 cup red soya-bean flour • 3/4 cup water • 2-1/4 cups sugar • 2 tablespoons lard or vegetable shortening • 1 cup rice flour • 3/4 all-purpose flour • 3/4 cup water • 1/2 cup sesame seeds • Oil for deep-frying

In China, these fried sesame sweets are offered to guests during certain festivals. At the time of the Chinese New Year, they are thought to bring good luck.

1. In a medium saucepan over medium heat, combine soya flour and 3/4 cup water; stir in sugar. Cook 10 minutes or until mixture begins to thicken. Remove from heat; cool mixture until a firm paste is formed.

2. In another saucepan, melt lard or shortening. Add cooled paste. Stir over low heat to blend, 1 to 2 minutes; cool mixture.

3. In a medium bowl, combine rice flour and all-purpose flour. Gradually add 3/4 cup water. Work into a pliable dough.

4. Using rice flour, lightly flour a work surface. Roll dough into a long log, about 1-1/2 inches in diameter.

5. Cut log into 25 to 30 (1-inch) pieces. Flatten each piece with the palm of your hand to make small circles.

6. Using the cooled soya paste, make 25 to 30 (1/2-inch) balls. Enclose each ball completely in a circle of dough, sealing well. Roll balls between your hands to smooth surface.

7. Spread sesame seeds in a shallow container. Roll balls in seeds, pressing lightly to make seeds stick. Balls can be lightly moistened if seeds do not stick.

8. Heat oil to 325 to 350F (165 to 175C) or until a 1-inch cube of bread turns golden brown in 65 seconds. Fry balls in hot oil until lightly browned. Makes 25 to 30 sweets.

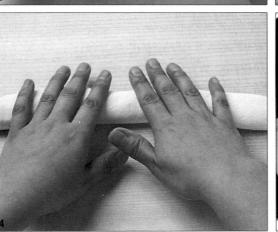

Almond Jelly

2 (1/4-oz.) pkgs. unflavored gelatin • 1/2 cup cold water • 2 cups hot water • 1 cup sugar • 1 cup milk • 1 teaspoon almond extract **Pureed Fruit Toppings:** 1/4 melon and 1 tablespoon sugar • 2 fresh or canned peaches, drained, and 1 tablespoon sugar

1. In a small saucepan, soak gelatin in cold water 5 minutes to soften.

2. Add hot water. Stir constantly over low heat until completely dissolved.

3. Add 1 cup sugar; stir until dissolved.

4. Add milk; cook until mixture nearly boils. Remove from heat immediately.

5. Stir in almond extract. Strain mixture, if desired.

6. Cool slightly, then pour into small glasses, filling them 1/2 to 3/4 full. Refrigerate until set. To serve, pour pureed fruit topping over each serving. Makes 6 to 8 servings.

Almond Jelly or *Shilen toufu* is served with a pureed fruit topping, usually melon or peach. This is made by processing each type of fruit separately with sugar in a blender.

Two-Color Lake Dessert

Chinese Cream: 2 tablespoons sesame seeds • 5 tablespoons all-purpose flour • 1 cup water • 5 tablespoons sugar
Colored Balls: 2/3 cup rice flour • 1/4 cup water • Red food coloring

1. For Chinese Cream, in a medium skillet, toast sesame seeds, being careful not to burn them. Place toasted sesame seeds in a blender; process until coarsely ground.

2. In a medium saucepan, heat flour over low heat until golden; cool completely.

3. Gradually add water to cooled flour, stirring over low heat. Add sugar, stirring constantly. Cook until cream thickens and the raw taste is gone.

4. Stir in ground toasted sesame seeds; keep warm over low heat.

5. For colored balls, combine rice flour and water in a medium bowl; stir until thick and blended.

6. Divide flour mixture in 1/2. To 1 part, add 2 to 3 drops of food coloring, blending until mixture is light pink.

7. Shape the pink mixture and the remaining white mixture into 1/2-inch balls.

8. Bring a medium saucepan of water to a boil. Add the balls; boil until balls come to the surface, about 10 minutes. Drain well.

9. Pour warm cream in a shallow serving dish. Float cooked balls in cream. Serve hot. Makes 4 to 6 servings.

This Chinese dessert is served hot. The colored balls floating in the cream give it the name. The Chinese Cream is used as a base in many other Chinese recipes.

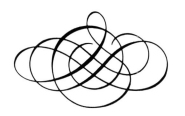

SWEET BREADS

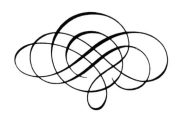

Panettone

2 (1/4-oz.) pkgs. active dry yeast (2 tablespoons) ● 1/2 cup warm water (110F, 45C) ● 1-1/4 cups sugar ●
7-1/2 to 8 cups all-purpose flour ● 1/2 teaspoon salt ● 1 cup butter or margarine, melted ● 5 egg yolks ● 2 eggs ●
1 cup warm milk ● 1 cup chopped candied fruit ● 1 cup raisins soaked in 2 tablespoons brandy

1. In a small bowl, combine yeast, water, 1 tablespoon sugar and 1 cup flour. Let stand 15 to 20 minutes or until foamy.

2. In a large bowl, combine yeast mixture, salt, butter or margarine, egg yolks, eggs, milk and remaining sugar. Add 6 cups flour. Beat until smooth. Add additional flour, if needed, to form a soft dough.

3. Turn out dough on a lightly floured surface. Knead about 10 minutes. Knead in candied fruit and raisins.

4. Cover and let rise in a warm place until doubled in bulk, about 3 hours.

5. Line 2 (7- or 8-inch) springform pans with waxed paper; grease well. Punch down dough. Shape into 2 round loaves. Place in prepared pans. Cover and let rise again until doubled in bulk, about 1-1/2 hours.

6. Preheat oven to 350F (175C). Make 2 slits in the top of each loaf in the shape of a cross. Brush lightly with butter or margarine. Bake 30 to 40 minutes or until it tests done. Makes 2 loaves.

Some experts maintain that Panettone originated in Como, not in Milan. However, in the 19th century, bakers in Lombardy used to give a Panettone to their customers at Christmas, thus establishing a tradition.

Kugelhupf

1 (1/4-oz.) pkg. active dry yeast (1 tablespoon) • 1/4 cup warm water (110F, 45C) • 3/4 cup powdered sugar •
1/4 cup milk • 2-1/2 to 2-3/4 cups all-purpose flour • 1 egg • 1/4 cup finely chopped candied fruit • 1/3 cup golden raisins •
1 teaspoon grated lemon peel • 1/2 cup butter or margarine • 3 egg yolks • 3 tablespoons coarsely chopped almonds •
1 egg blended with 1 teaspoon powdered sugar for glaze • Powdered sugar

1. Dissolve yeast in warm water with 1 teaspoon of sugar. Let stand until foamy. In a medium bowl, combine milk, 1-1/2 cups flour, 1 egg and yeast mixture. Stir in candied fruit, raisins and lemon peel. Let stand while completing next step.

2. In a separate bowl, blend butter or margarine, powdered sugar and egg yolks.

3. Stir in yeast mixture. Beat in enough remaining flour to make a soft dough. Knead 4 to 5 minutes.

4. Cover and let rise in a warm place until doubled in bulk, about 3 hours.

5. Butter an 8-inch kugelhupf mold. Press chopped nuts onto side of mold. Place dough in prepared mold. Cover and let rise until doubled in bulk, 30 to 45 minutes.

6. Preheat oven to 350F (175C). Bake 40 to 50 minutes. Unmold while still hot and place on a wire rack. Brush with egg glaze. To serve, sprinkle with powdered sugar. Makes 1 (8-inch) ring.

The basic dough for this recipe makes a plain ring cake. By adding extra ingredients, a wide variety of rings can be created. Saxon Ring Cake contains aniseed. Cherry Ring Cake is an American favorite. Hamburg Ring Cake contains almonds, cinnamon, candied fruit and ginger. Bremen Ring Cake is similar to a fruitcake, though still ring-shaped. Dutch Steamed Ring Cake is cooked in a cloth like a Christmas pudding. French Trianon Ring Cake is filled with chocolate cream and covered with chocolate icing.

Fruit Ring Bread

Dough: 1 (1/4-oz.) pkg. active dry yeast (1 tablespoon) ● 1/4 cup warm water (110F, 45C) ● 2 tablespoons ground almonds ● 3/4 cup milk ● 4 to 4-1/2 cups all-purpose flour ● 1/2 cup sugar ● 2 egg yolks ● 1 egg ● 1/4 cup butter or margarine, room temperature ● 1 teaspoon vanilla extract ● 1 teaspoon ground cinnamon ● 1/2 cup raisins ● 1/2 cup chopped candied fruit ● 2 tablespoons chopped candied cherries **Rum Glaze:** 1/2 cup powdered sugar ● 2 to 3 teaspoons rum **Decoration:** Walnut halves ● Candied fruit ● Candied cherries

1. For dough, dissolve yeast in water. In a large bowl, combine almonds with milk. Stir in 2 cups flour, sugar, egg yolks, egg, butter or margarine and vanilla. Beat well. Blend in yeast mixture. Add enough remaining flour to make a soft dough.

2. Place dough on a lightly floured surface. Add cinnamon; knead until cinnamon is blended in. Cover and let rise in a warm place until doubled in bulk, 1-1/2 to 2 hours.

3. Punch down dough. Flatten dough with your hands. Sprinkle raisins, candied fruit and candied cherries on top.

4. Form dough into a ball with fruit inside. Generously butter a straight-sided 8- or 9-inch ring mold.

5. Shape dough to fit mold. Press into buttered mold. Cover and let rise in a warm place until doubled in bulk, about 45 minutes.

6. Preheat oven to 350F (175C). Bake 30 to 35 minutes or until done. If top browns too quickly, cover with foil. Remove from oven. Cool on a wire rack. For glaze, in a small bowl, combine sugar and rum. Spoon glaze over cake, allowing it to run down the side. Before glaze becomes firm, decorate with walnuts, candied fruit and candied cherries. Makes 1 (8- or 9-inch) bread.

Carrot Ring Cake

Cake: 1/2 cup grated carrot • 1/3 cup sugar • 3 eggs, separated • 1/3 cup all-purpose flour • 1/2 cup ground almonds •
1 teaspoon grated lemon peel • 1 tablespoon lemon juice • 1/4 to 1/2 cup orange liqueur
Kirsch Butter Cream: 1/4 cup powdered sugar • 1/4 cup butter or margarine, room temperature • 1 egg yolk •
1 tablespoon kirsch   **Decoration:** Chantilly Cream, page 195

This recipe is a variation of one of the most famous types of
carrot cake, made in the state of Aargau in Switzerland. It is
sometimes covered with chocolate icing. The Aargau carrot cake
is covered with kirsch-flavored icing and is decorated with
chopped, toasted almonds, then sprinkled with powdered sugar.

1. Preheat oven to 350F (175C). Butter and lightly flour a 6- to 8-cup ring mold.

2. Finely grate carrot.

3. Place sugar, egg yolks and flour in a double boiler over hot water. Beat until mixture thickens.

4. Remove from heat; stir in grated carrot, almonds, lemon peel and lemon juice.

5. Beat egg whites until stiff but not dry.

6. Fold egg whites carefully into carrot mixture.

7. Pour 1/2 the batter into prepared mold. Prepare the Kirsch Butter Cream, see Liqueur-Butter Cream, page 195. Spread over surface, then cover with remaining batter.

8. Bake 45 minutes or until cake tests done. Unmold; brush top with orange liqueur. Decorate with Chantilly Cream. Makes 1 cake.

Fruit Cake

1 cup plus 2 tablespoons butter ● 2-1/4 cups powdered sugar ● 4 eggs, separated ● 1-3/4 cups all-purpose flour ●
1 teaspoon baking powder ● 1/2 teaspoon salt ● 1-1/2 cups raisins ● 1/3 cup rum ● 1 cup chopped candied fruit

The fruit cake was an English invention and is famous all over
the world. The basic recipe can be adapted to give a range of
variations by adding chopped nuts or other chopped dried or
candied fruits. Ginger Cake is another version of the same
recipe that differs from other versions in that it contains no nuts
or fruit, but is flavored with ginger.

1. Cream butter until light and smooth.

2. Beat in powdered sugar, a little at a time.

3. Beat egg whites until stiff but not dry. Stir 1/2 the beaten egg whites into butter mixture. Then fold in remaining egg whites.

4. Add egg yolks, blending well.

5. Stir flour, baking powder and salt into mixture. Allow mixture to rest.

6. Meanwhile, soak raisins in rum about 30 minutes. Stir soaked raisins with any remaining rum and candied fruit into batter.

7. Preheat oven to 350F (175C). Grease a 9'' x 5'' x 3'' loaf pan; line with waxed paper. Grease the paper. Pour batter into lined pan. Smooth surface with a spatula.

8. Bake 45 to 55 minutes or until cake tests done. Cool on a wire rack. Slice to serve. Makes 1 loaf.

TIP: If cake is dry, sprinkle lightly with rum. Wrap in a cloth or plastic bag and let stand until moistened throughout. Repeat as desired.

Orange Cake

1 cup powdered sugar ● 2/3 cup butter, room temperature ● 2 eggs ● 1 teaspoon grated orange peel ●
1/2 teaspoon vanilla extract ● 1 cup all-purpose flour ● 1/2 teaspoon baking powder ● 1 orange

This recipe is a variation of the preceeding fruit cake but uses
fresh fruit rather than dried or candied fruit. The mixture rises
more and is softer and less dense. The method and ingredients
can be used to make many other delicious cakes with a variety of
fresh fruit.

1. Grease and flour an 8'' x 4'' loaf pan.

2. Sift sugar into a small bowl.

3. In a medium bowl, cream butter until light and smooth.

4. Gradually add sifted sugar, blending well.

5. Lightly beat eggs; stir into butter mixture.

6. Stir in orange peel and vanilla.

7. Stir in flour and baking powder.

8. Peel the orange. Separate into segments; remove seeds and membrane, if desired. Pour 1/3 the batter into prepared pan. Arrange 1/2 the orange segments on top. Pour in another 1/3 of the batter. Cover with remaining orange segments. Add remaining batter. Let stand about 30 minutes. Preheat oven to 350F (175C). Bake 60 minutes or until cake tests done. Makes 1 loaf cake.

Brioche

1 (1/4-oz.) pkg. active dry yeast (1 tablespoon) • 1/4 cup warm water (110F, 45C) • 1/4 cup sugar •
2-1/2 cups all-purpose flour • 3/4 cup butter or margarine • 1 teaspoon salt • 3 eggs • 1 beaten egg for glaze

This classic brioche is baked in round fluted tins. Brioches can be
made in many different shapes and, although the dough is the
same, they are named according to their shape.

1. In a small bowl, combine yeast, water, 1 tablespoon sugar and 1/4 cup flour. Let stand 15 to 20 minutes or until foamy.

2. In a medium bowl, cream butter or margarine.

3. In a large bowl, combine remaining flour, sugar and salt. Add eggs; work into a paste.

4. When paste is smooth, add yeast mixture from step 1.

5. Work in creamed butter from step 2. Dough will be soft. Beat or knead in the bowl 5 to 10 minutes. Cover and let stand in a warm place until doubled in bulk, 2 to 3 hours.

6. Divide dough into 2 pieces; the smaller piece should be about 1/4 of the dough. Grease brioche pans or desired pan. Divide each piece of dough into 6 to 10 equal pieces depending on pan size. Place the larger pieces of dough in greased pans. Make an indentation in center of each ball; moisten lightly with water. Make small pear-shaped balls. Place small-end down in indentation in center of each large ball.

7. Or, if desired, pinch off a quarter of each dough ball, then make a dip in the center with the fingers and place a tiny ball of dough from the remaining quarter in the dip.

8. Cover and let rise in a warm place until doubled in bulk, 30 to 40 minutes. Preheat oven to 425F (220C). Place pans on a baking sheet. Brush brioches with beaten egg. Bake 10 to 20 minutes or until golden. Remove from oven. Unmold and allow to cool. Makes 6 (4-inch) or 10 (3-inch) brioches. Dough can also be used to make 1 large brioche.

Brioche Croissants

1 (1/4-oz.) pkg. active dry yeast (1 tablespoon) ● 1/4 cup warm water (110F, 45C) ● 3 tablespoons sugar ●
2-1/2 cups all-purpose flour ● 1/2 teaspoon salt ● 1 egg ● 1 egg yolk ● 1/3 cup milk ● 1/4 cup butter or margarine ●
1/2 to 3/4 cup butter or margarine, room temperature ● 1 egg beaten with 1 teaspoon powdered sugar for glaze

Croissants, like brioches, are of French origin but are known all
over the world. The main difference between croissants and
brioches is the crescent shape of the croissants. They can also be
filled with cream or jam, as are the German Kipfel. This recipe is
entitled Brioche Croissants. In France it would simply be
Croissants since croissants are generally made with a brioche
dough and are smooth, soft and light. Croissants can also be
made with Flaky Pastry, page 196.

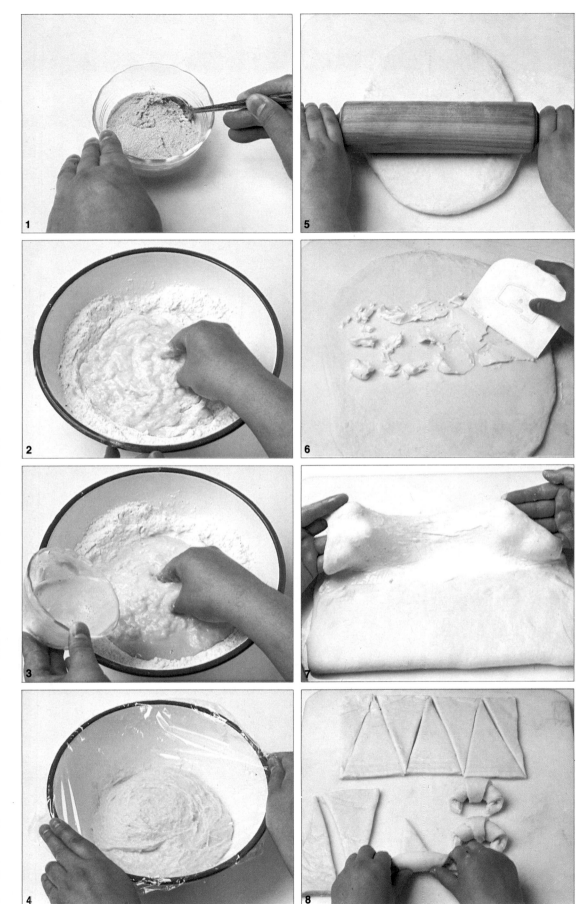

1. In a small bowl, combine yeast, water, 1 tablespoon sugar and 1/4 cup flour. Let stand 15 to 20 minutes or until foamy.

2. Place remaining flour in a large bowl. Make a well in center of flour. Blend in remaining sugar, salt, egg, egg yolk, milk and 1/4 cup butter or margarine.

3. Add yeast mixture from step 1; blend thoroughly. Turn out on a lightly floured board. Clean and grease bowl. Knead dough 5 minutes. Then place in greased bowl, turning dough once to grease well.

4. Cover and let rise in a warm place until doubled in bulk, about 1-1/2 hours.

5. Roll out dough to about 12'' x 9''.

6. Spread 1/2 to 3/4 cup butter or margarine over 2/3 of the dough.

7. Fold dough in thirds; roll out again. Refrigerate 15 minutes. Fold in thirds again and roll out. Refrigerate another 15 minutes.

8. Butter and flour a baking sheet. Roll out dough to a 15'' x 8'' rectangle 1/2 to 3/4 inch thick. Cut into 2 (15'' x 4'') rectangles. Cut each rectangle into triangles. Starting from the wide base, roll up each triangle. Curve into a crescent shape. Place on prepared baking sheet. Brush with glaze mixture. Let rise in a cool place until doubled in bulk. Preheat oven to 425F (220C). Bake 15 to 20 minutes. Makes 10 to 12 croissants.

Raisin Bread

3 (1/4-oz) pkgs. active dry yeast (3 tablespoons) ● 1/2 cup warm water (110F, 45C) ● 8 cups all-purpose flour ●
1-1/4 cups sugar ● 1 teaspoon salt ● 3/4 cup butter, room temperature ● 3/4 to 1 cup warm milk ●
1 cup raisins soaked in 1/2 cup Marsala ● 3/4 cup chopped nuts ● 1/2 cup chopped candied orange peel or lemon peel

1. Dissolve yeast in warm water.

2. Sift flour, sugar and salt into a bowl; make a well in center. Add yeast mixture, butter and 3/4 cup warm milk. Work into a dough. Add more milk, if necessary, to make a soft dough. Work in raisins, nuts and candied peel.

3. Knead 15 to 20 minutes. Place in a greased bowl, turning once.

4. Cover and let rise in a warm place 2 to 3 hours or until doubled in bulk.

5. Preheat oven to 350F (175C). Butter a baking sheet. Shape dough in 2 round loaves. Place on buttered baking sheet. Make 3 triangular cuts on the top of each loaf. This is the traditional way of marking this bread, like the 2 crosses on the Panettone. Bake 45 to 50 minutes. Makes 2 loaves.

Raisin bread is a traditional Italian sweet that is made for Christmas, New Year and Epiphany in Liguria. Its fame has spread far beyond Italian shores and it is more commonly known as *Genoese sweet bread*. Another well-known variety is made with raisins, but without nuts.

COOKIES

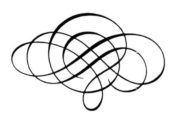

Ladyfingers

3/4 cup granulated sugar • 6 eggs, separated • 1-3/4 cups all-purpose flour • 1 teaspoon salt • 1/4 cup powdered sugar • 1/4 cup granulated sugar

1. Preheat oven to 325F (165C). Grease a baking sheet.

2. Beat 3/4 cup sugar and egg yolks until creamy. Continuing to beat, gradually add flour and salt.

3. Beat egg whites until stiff but not dry. Stir 1/3 of beaten egg whites into batter until soft. Fold in remaining beaten egg whites.

4. Using a piping bag with a wide plain tip, pipe dough into 4-inch strips on greased baking sheet. Allow room to spread.

5. Blend powdered sugar and 1/4 cup granulated sugar. Sprinkle over fingers.

6. Bake 15 to 20 minutes or until done. Cool on a wire rack. Makes about 60.

Scones

5 cups all-purpose flour • 1 teaspoon baking powder • 1/2 teaspoon salt • 1 tablespoon grated orange peel or lemon peel •
6 tablespoons butter or margarine, room temperature • 1/4 cup plus 2 tablespoons sugar • 1 egg •
1-1/2 cups half and half or milk • 1 beaten egg for glaze

1. Sift together flour, baking powder and salt into a large bowl.

2. Add orange or lemon peel. Work in butter or margarine.

3. Add sugar; blend well.

4. Add 1 egg and half and half or milk. Knead lightly to make a soft dough.

5. Cover dough with plastic wrap. Let stand about 1 hour.

6. Preheat oven to 400F (205C). Grease a baking sheet. Roll out dough until 3/4 inch thick. Cut out scones with a pastry cutter. Place on greased baking sheet. Brush scones lightly with egg glaze. Bake 10 to 12 minutes. Makes about 18 (2-1/2-inch) scones.

Although the basic recipe for scones uses only flour, baking powder, butter, milk and a pinch of salt, this recipe is enriched with eggs and cream. Scones are eaten warm or cold either at breakfast or tea-time. They are usually spread with butter and jam, or served with cheese. Variations on the basic recipe include cheese scones and scones with dried fruit or candied peel.

Almond Macaroons

4 cups finely ground blanched almonds • 1-1/2 cups sugar • 1 teaspoon vanilla extract • 3 egg whites

1. Preheat oven to 300F (150C). Grease and flour a baking sheet.

2. In a medium bowl, combine almonds, sugar and vanilla. Stir in egg whites, 1 at a time, to make a soft, well-blended paste.

3. Using a piping bag fitted with a round plain tip, pipe 1- to 2-inch drops of dough on greased baking sheet.

4. Bake cookies 20 to 30 minutes or until done. Makes about 36 cookies.

Some people, misled by the fact that the industrial production of macaroons began in Lombardy in Italy, regard the macaroon as a Lombard sweet. In fact, the macaroon was originally made in Sicily although it is now eaten world-wide. Descended from the Sicilian macaroon and equally well-known, at least in Europe, is the Coburg macaroon from Upper Bavaria. It contains whole eggs, honey, cocoa, spices, hazelnut flour and candied peel. In France, macaroons are decorated with royal icing.

Cheese Straws

2/3 cup butter or margarine, room temperature • 1/2 cup grated sharp Cheddar cheese (1-1/2 oz.) • 1 egg, beaten • 1/4 cup milk • 1-1/2 cups all-purpose flour • 1/4 teaspoon ground nutmeg • 1/4 teaspoon white pepper • 1/4 teaspoon salt

1. Preheat oven to 350F (175C). Grease a baking sheet.

2. Cream butter or margarine until light colored.

3. Blend cheese with butter or margarine.

4. Stir egg into cheese mixture.

5. Gradually stir in milk, blending well.

6. Add flour, nutmeg, pepper and salt; blend well.

7. Spoon mixture into a piping bag with a fluted or star-shaped tip. Pipe 3- to 4-inch strips onto greased baking sheet.

8. Bake 10 to 15 minutes. Cool on a wire rack. Makes 75 to 80, depending on size.

Cheese straws can be made with Cheddar, Cheshire or any leftover hard cheese. In Switzerland, there is a similar recipe made with Sbrinz cheese. Cheese straws are generally eaten with cocktails or as a snack.

Cut-Out Cookies & Rolled Chocolate Cookies

For Cut-Out Cookies: 1/2 cup butter, room temperature ● 2/3 cup sugar ● 4 egg yolks ●
1/2 teaspoon baking powder and 1/4 teaspoon cream of tartar, or 3 cream of tartar tablets ●
2 cups all-purpose flour ● 1/2 teaspoon salt ● Large crystal sugar

To make Cut-Out Cookies:

1. Preheat oven to 350F (175C). Grease a baking sheet. Cream butter until light and pale.

2. Stir in sugar; blend well.

3. Add egg yolks, 1 at a time.

4. Stir thoroughly until all ingredients are blended.

5. If using cream of tartar tablets, crush with a rolling pin.

6. Sift baking powder and cream of tartar with flour and salt.

Continued on next page.

7

11

8

12

9

13

10

14

7. Add dry ingredients to butter mixture.

8. Blend well.

9. As mixture becomes more difficult to work, stir with a wooden spoon until well blended. Mixture will be quite crumbly.

10. Cover and let stand a few minutes. Do not refrigerate.

11. Lightly flour a work surface.

12. To avoid pastry breaking up because it is so crumbly, work pastry in 3 separate pieces.

13. Make a ball or block of each of the 3 pieces of pastry. Sprinkle lightly with flour.

14. Roll out dough with a rolling pin.

15. If the sheets of pastry stick to the board, use a broad spatula or dough scraper to free them.

16. Roll out dough to about 1/4 inch thick.

17. Cut dough into shapes with decorative cutters.

18. Dip both sides of each cookie in crystal sugar. Place on greased baking sheet. Bake 10 to 15 minutes or until lightly browned. Makes 48 to 60 cookies, depending on size.

15

For Rolled Chocolate Cookies:
2 cups all-purpose flour ● 1/4 teaspoon salt ●
1/2 teaspoon baking soda ● 1 teaspoon baking powder ●
1/4 cup sugar ● 1 teaspoon ginger, if desired ●
5 tablespoons sugar ● 1/4 cup water ●
1 tablespoon liqueur ● 3 to 4 oz. semisweet chocolate ●
6 tablespoons butter ● Royal Icing, if desired, page 195

16

19

17

20

To make Rolled Chocolate Cookies:

19. Sift together flour, salt, baking soda, baking powder, 1/4 cup sugar and ginger, if desired. In a small saucepan, combine 5 tablespoons sugar, 1/4 cup water and 1 tablespoon liqueur. Dissolve over low heat to make a syrup.

20. Melt chocolate and butter in a double boiler over low heat. Add melted chocolate and butter to dry ingredients from step 19. Add 1/4 cup sugar syrup from step 19. Add more syrup, if needed. Work together to form a smooth dough. Cover and let stand 30 minutes.

21. Preheat oven to 350F (175C). Grease a baking sheet. Roll out dough until 1/4 inch thick. Cut out dough using desired cookie cutters. Place cookies on greased baking sheet. Bake 12 to 15 minutes. Remove from oven. Cool on baking sheet 2 to 3 minutes before removing to a wire rack. Decorate with Royal Icing, if desired. Makes 18 to 48 cookies, depending on size.

18

21

Jam Drops

2/3 cup butter, room temperature ● 3/4 cup sugar ● 2 eggs ● 1 teaspoon grated lemon peel ● 2 tablespoons Marsala ●
1-1/2 cups all-purpose flour ● 2 to 3 tablespoons sugar ● 1/4 cup apricot jam

1. Cream butter in a bowl. Gradually add 3/4 cup sugar. Stir in eggs, lemon peel and Marsala, blending well. Sift flour in gradually, stirring until well blended. If dough is too stiff, add a little more Marsala.

2. Cover and refrigerate dough 2 hours.

3. Preheat oven to 350F (175C). Grease a baking sheet. Using your hands, shape dough in small balls about the size of walnuts. Roll in 2 to 3 tablespoons sugar. Place on greased baking sheet. Flatten each with the base of a glass dipped in flour to make cookies about 1-1/4 inches in diameter.

4. Using your finger, make a well in the center of each cookie. Fill each with a teaspoon of jam.

5. Bake 15 minutes or until done. Makes about 20 cookies.

Peanut Cookies

2/3 cup butter, room temperature • 1/4 cup granulated sugar • 1/4 cup packed brown sugar •
2/3 cup ground dry roasted peanuts • 1 egg • 1 teaspoon grated orange peel • 1-1/4 cups all-purpose flour •
1/4 teaspoon baking powder • 1 egg yolk, slightly beaten

1. In a medium bowl, cream together butter and sugars. Stir in peanuts. Add 1 egg and orange peel. Blend well. Stir in flour and baking powder.

2. Cover and refrigerate 30 minutes.

3. Preheat oven to 350F (175C). Grease a baking sheet.

4. Roll out dough to 1/4 inch thick on a lightly floured surface. Dip a cookie cutter about 1-1/2 to 2 inches in diameter in flour. Cut out cookies. Place on greased baking sheet. Using a fork, make a crisscross pattern on top of each cookie. Brush cookies lightly with egg yolk.

5. Bake 15 minutes or until done. Makes about 30 cookies.

Almond Paste Rings & Stars

7 tablespoons butter, room temperature   •   1-1/4 cups sugar   •   3-1/2 cups ground almonds   •   1 egg   •   2 egg whites   •
1 teaspoon grated lemon peel or orange peel   •   Few tablespoons cornstarch   •   1/2 cup chopped candied fruit

Where almond paste is concerned, the patisserie of Sicily leads
the way. This recipe is only one of the many uses for this paste.
Almond paste originated in Sicily, with its age-old tradition of
patisserie, and is now known all over the world.

1. In a medium bowl, cream together butter and sugar.

2. Add almonds; blend well.

3. Beat in 1 egg. Then beat in egg whites, 1 at a time.

4. Stir in lemon or orange peel.

5. If the dough is too soft, add a few tablespoons cornstarch until pastry is firm.

6. Place dough in a piping bag fitted with a star-shaped tip about 1/2 inch wide.

7. Grease a baking sheet. Pipe dough onto greased baking sheet. For ring-shaped cookies, pipe dough in a circle with ends overlapping. For star-shaped cookies, pipe directly onto sheet, pulling bag straight up.

8. Press candied-fruit pieces onto each cookie, as desired. Let stand 5 to 6 hours. Preheat oven to 350F (175C). Bake cookies 15 minutes or until lightly golden. Makes 36 to 40 cookies.

Chocolate-Chip Cookies & Oatmeal Cookies

For Chocolate-Chip Cookies: 1/3 cup butter or margarine, room temperature ● 3/4 cup sugar ●
1/4 teaspoon vanilla extract ● 1-1/4 cups all-purpose flour ● 1/2 teaspoon salt ● 1 teaspoon baking powder ●
1 egg, slightly beaten ● 4 to 6 oz. semisweet or milk chocolate pieces ● 1/2 cup chopped walnuts

Some cookies made with flour, sugar and eggs are so simple,
even a child could make them. To the basic recipe for these
cookies, a great range of ingredients can be added. Replace the
chocolate pieces with raisins, coconut, chopped dates, chopped
candied fruit or peanuts.

For Oatmeal Cookies:
1/2 cup butter or margarine ●
1/2 cup brown sugar ● 1/4 cup granulated sugar ●
1/4 teaspoon vanilla extract ● 1 cup all-purpose flour ●
1/2 teaspoon salt ● 1/2 teaspoon baking soda ●
1 egg, beaten ● 1 cup rolled oats, toasted ●
1/2 cup chopped walnuts

To make Chocolate-Chip Cookies:

1. Preheat oven to 350F (175C). Grease a baking sheet. Cream together butter or margarine, sugar and vanilla.

2. Stir in flour, salt and baking powder.

3. Add beaten egg, stirring well to blend.

4. Stir in chocolate pieces and nuts.

5. Drop dough by teaspoonfuls onto greased baking sheet. Bake 10 to 12 minutes or until lightly browned. Cool on wire racks. Makes about 40 cookies.

To make Oatmeal Cookies:

6. Combine the ingredients following steps 1, 2 and 3.

7. Grind rolled oats in a blender or food processor until fine crumbs. Stir in ground rolled oats and walnuts. Follow step 5 for baking instructions.

Almond Drops

1/2 cup plus 1 tablespoon butter or margarine, room temperature ● 1/2 cup sugar ● 1-2/3 cups all-purpose flour ●
1/8 teaspoon almond extract ● 1/2 teaspoon salt ● 1 egg ● 1 egg yolk blended with 1 tablespoon water for glaze ●
25 to 30 almond halves

Almonds are the undisputed monarchs of European pastries.
They are used with great frequency in all kinds of desserts,
creams and cookies. They can be toasted, salted and eaten with
cocktails. They can be pralined or caramelized or used in
confections. They are an essential ingredient in nougat,
marzipan, almond paste and almond milk.

146

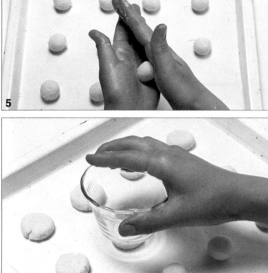

1. Cream butter or margarine in a bowl.

2. Beat in sugar, a little at a time.

3. Blend in flour, almond extract and salt.

4. Add egg; work to a smooth paste. Refrigerate dough 2 hours or until firm.

5. Preheat oven to 350F (175C). Grease a baking sheet. With your hands, shape dough into 1-inch balls. Place on greased baking sheet.

6. Flatten each ball with the base of a custard cup or drinking glass.

7. Brush with egg-yolk glaze.

8. Place an almond half on each cookie. Bake 10 minutes. Cool on a wire rack. Makes 25 to 28 cookies.

147

Cats' Tongues

1/2 cup plus 1 tablespoon butter, room temperature ● 1-1/2 cups all-purpose flour ● 1-1/4 cups powdered sugar ●
1/4 teaspoon vanilla extract ● 2 or 3 egg whites

1. Preheat oven to 350F (175C). Heavily grease a baking sheet.

2. Cream butter in a bowl.

3. Beating constantly, sift in flour and sugar. Stir in vanilla.

4. Beat 2 egg whites until stiff but not dry; fold carefully into butter mixture. If dough is not soft enough, add another beaten egg white. Dough will look grainy and rough.

5. Spoon dough into a piping bag fitted with a wide plain tip.

6. Pipe dough into 3-1/2- to 4-inch pieces, 2 inches apart, on greased baking sheet.

7. Bake 8 to 10 minutes. Cookies are done when edges begin to turn golden brown. Makes 42 to 48 cookies.

Mother-In-Laws' Tongues

1/2 cup half and half ● 2 eggs, separated ● 2-1/4 cups powdered sugar ● 3/4 cup all-purpose flour ● 1 teaspoon baking powder ● 1-3/4 cups sliced, blanched almonds

1. In a medium bowl, beat together half and half and egg yolks.

2. Sift together sugar, flour and baking powder; blend into half-and-half mixture.

3. In a small bowl, whisk egg whites until stiff. Carefully fold egg whites into half-and-half mixture. Let stand several hours.

4. Preheat oven to 350F (175C). Grease and flour a heavy baking sheet. If baking sheet is not heavy enough, base of cookies will burn. Spoon dough into a piping bag fitted with a plain nozzle about 1 inch wide and 1/4 inch thick. Pipe onto prepared baking sheet in 2-inch-long strips, spacing 2 inches apart.

5. Cover each strip with 1/2 tablespoon sliced almonds.

6. Bake 5 minutes; immediately remove from baking sheet. Cool on a wire rack. To make cookies rounded, press over a rolling pin while still warm. Makes about 60 cookies.

Tea Cookies

For Plain Cookies: 3/4 cup plus 2 tablespoons butter, room temperature ● 3/4 cup powdered sugar ● 1 egg white ●
1-3/4 cups all-purpose flour, sifted ● 1 teaspoon baking powder

To make Plain Cookies:

1. Cream butter and sugar. Beat egg white until stiff but not dry; fold in carefully.

2. Add flour and baking powder; blend well.

3. Cover and let stand 1 hour.

4. Knead dough lightly on a floured surface.

5. Roll dough into cylinders about 1-1/2 inches in diameter; wrap in plastic wrap. Refrigerate until well chilled.

6. Preheat oven to 350F (175C). Grease a baking sheet. Cut chilled dough into 1/2-inch slices with a sharp knife. Place on greased baking sheet. Bake 8 to 10 minutes. Keep a careful watch as they will begin to brown very quickly. Makes about 40 cookies.

Other cookies on next page.

For Two-Colored Squares:
1/2 cup plus 2 tablespoons butter, room temperature •
1-1/2 cups powdered sugar • 4 egg yolks •
1/2 teaspoon vanilla extract •
1-3/4 cups all-purpose flour •
1 teaspoon baking powder •
1/4 cup unsweetened cocoa powder •
1 egg yolk blended with 1 tablespoon water for glaze •
1/4 cup granulated sugar

To make Two-Colored Squares:

7. Make a dough with all the ingredients except cocoa, egg-yolk glaze and granulated sugar. If dough is too soft, add more flour. Divide off 1/3 of the dough. Add cocoa to remaining dough.

8. Roll light-colored dough into an 8-inch-long cylinder. Roll 1/2 the dark dough into an 8-inch-long cylinder. Flatten both cylinders, light and dark, as shown.

9. Cut flattened pieces in half lengthwise.

10. With remaining dark dough, roll out a rectangle large enough to enclose all the cylinders once. Brush dough with egg-yolk glaze. Place 1 of the cylinders 3/4 the way down the sheet of dough; brush with egg-yolk glaze. Place a second cylinder of different color dough next to the first. Brush with egg-yolk glaze.

11. Place remaining 2 cylinders on top, alternating colors and brushing with glaze.

12. Roll cylinders in outer dough. Cut away any excess. Chill logs, if needed. Sprinkle dough log with granulated sugar. Preheat oven to 350F (175C). Grease a baking sheet.

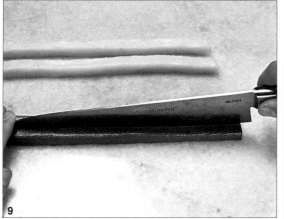

13. Cut chilled dough in 1/4-inch slices. Place slices on greased baking sheet. Bake about 10 minutes. Makes about 40 cookies.

For Coconut Fingers:

1-1/2 cups packed shredded coconut •
3/4 cup butter, room temperature • 3/4 cup sugar •
1 egg • 2 cups all-purpose flour •
1 teaspoon baking powder •
1 egg yolk blended with 1 tablespoon water for glaze •
Shredded coconut for decoration •
Cinnamon mixed with sugar to sprinkle over cookies

To make Coconut Fingers:

14. Spread 1-1/2 cups coconut on a baking sheet; toast in a 275F (135C) oven until coconut begins to brown lightly. Stir occasionally. Be careful not to let coconut brown excessively. Cool; grind coconut in blender.

15. Cream butter, then beat in sugar followed by egg.

16. Sift flour and baking powder; gradually stir into egg mixture. Add ground coconut from step 14; blend well.

17. Place a piece of plastic wrap on a baking sheet or an 8- or 9-inch-square pan. Spread dough 1/2 inch thick on plastic wrap.

18. Smooth top carefully; trim corners and edges. Brush with egg-yolk glaze. Sprinkle with shredded coconut.

19. Sprinkle surface with cinnamon sugar. Cover with sheet of plastic wrap. Freeze until firm.

20. Preheat oven to 325F (165C). Grease a baking sheet. Remove plastic wrap from frozen dough. Place dough on a board. Cut into 2" x 1/2" strips. Place on greased baking sheet. Bake 12 to 15 minutes. Cool on a wire rack. Makes 60 cookies.

153

Almond Crackers

2 egg whites • 2 tablespoons cornstarch • 1/2 cup powdered sugar • 1/2 cup finely ground, blanched almonds

1. Preheat oven to 425F (220C). Line a baking sheet with parchment paper or greased foil. Beat egg whites until soft peaks form.

2. Sift cornstarch and sugar over beaten egg whites; beat until stiff peaks form.

3. Blend in almonds until smooth.

4. A form for the cookies can be made from 1/8-inch cardboard, then cover with foil. Using a 4'' x 2'' cookie form, place about 1 tablespoon batter in each form.

5. Smooth with a spatula until 1/8 inch thick. Cookies can also be made by shaping 1 tablespoon batter into a rectangle with a spatula.

6. Bake cookies 5 minutes; immediately remove from baking sheet. If cookies cool, reheat briefly for easy removal. Cool on a wire rack. Cookies are very fragile. Makes 30 to 36 cookies.

Almond Crescents

1 cup almonds, coarsely chopped ● 2/3 cup butter, room temperature ● 1/2 cup powdered sugar ● 1/4 cup Marsala ●
1-1/2 cups all-purpose flour

There are thousands of different recipes for almond cookies the
world over. The ingredients given here can be made into any
shape you like.

1. Preheat oven to 300F (150C). Toast almonds on a baking sheet 15 minutes. Stir occasionally during toasting. Cool almonds.

2. In a large bowl, cream together butter and sugar.

3. Stir in Marsala.

4. Add flour and toasted almonds; stir until well blended.

5. Let dough stand 30 minutes. Refrigerate if needed to handle easily.

6. Preheat oven to 350F (175C). Grease a baking sheet. Shape dough into a large log. Cut into 3 or 4 pieces. Roll out each piece to a long log. Cut into small pieces.

7. Shape each piece into a small log.

8. Curve each piece into a crescent. Place on greased baking sheet. Bake 15 to 18 minutes or until done. Makes about 20 cookies.

Madeleines

1/3 cup butter ● 2/3 cup powdered sugar ● 2 eggs, separated ● 2 tablespoons brandy or dark rum ●
1/4 teaspoon vanilla extract ● 1/2 cup cake flour ● 1/8 teaspoon salt

This is a classic French recipe from Alsace. The traditional molds
are shell-shaped. Smaller molds are often used, the resulting
cookies being called *madeleinettes*. When cooled, madeleines or
madeleinettes can be dusted with powdered sugar.

1. Preheat oven to 375F (190C). Brush madeleine molds with a little melted butter.

2. Melt 1/3 cup butter over hot water.

3. Sift sugar to eliminate lumps.

4. In a double boiler over simmering water, blend sugar, egg yolks and brandy or rum. Stir until warmed and thick. Pour into another bowl to cool.

5. Beat egg whites until stiff but not dry.

6. Blend in vanilla, flour and salt.

7. Add melted butter from step 2, then the mixture from step 4. Blend well.

8. Pour batter into buttered molds. Bake 10 minutes. Remove from molds at once. Cool on a wire rack, shell-side up. Makes about 12 madeleines.

Vanilla Crescents

2/3 cup butter, room temperature • 1/2 teaspoon vanilla extract • 2 cups sifted cake flour • 3/4 cup ground almonds •
1/4 cup granulated sugar • Powdered sugar

1. Preheat oven to 375F (190C). Grease a baking sheet.

2. Cream butter until pale and fluffy. Blend in vanilla.

3. Sift flour into a separate bowl. Blend in almonds and 1/4 cup sugar. Add flour mixture to creamed butter; blend until smooth.

4. Shape dough into rolls about 1/2 inch thick. Cut dough into 2-inch pieces. Roll in powdered sugar.

5. Place dough pieces on greased baking sheet, curving into deep crescents or horseshoe shapes.

6. Bake 10 to 12 minutes.

7. Remove from oven. Gently roll cookies in powdered sugar. These cookies are very fragile. Makes 24 cookies.

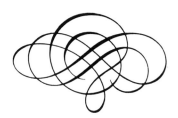

CREAMS, MOUSSES, SOUFFLÉS & ICE CREAM

Crème Caramel

1/2 cup sugar • 1/4 cup water • 2 cups milk • 1/3 cup sugar • 1/2 teaspoon vanilla extract • 2 eggs • 2 egg yolks • Chantilly Cream, page 195, if desired • Canned apricots, if desired

1. In a small heavy saucepan, heat 1/2 cup sugar and water until sugar dissolves. Boil until light brown.

2. Pour into an 8-cup soufflé dish or 8 custard cups. Immediately turn dish or cups to coat base and sides evenly with caramel; set aside.

3. In a medium saucepan, heat milk until surface shimmers. Stir in 1/3 cup sugar until dissolved; let cool 10 minutes. Stir in vanilla.

4. Preheat oven to 350F (175C). In a medium bowl, beat eggs and egg yolks until blended. Stir in milk mixture.

5. Pour into caramel-lined dish or cups. Place in a bain marie, page 187. Water should be boiling.

6. Bake 40 to 50 minutes in soufflé dish and 20 to 25 minutes in custard cups or until a knife inserted in center comes out clean.

7. Cool completely; turn out onto dessert plates. Top with Chantilly Cream and fruit, if desired. Makes 8 servings.

Coffee Gelatin & Wine Gelatin

Gelatin Mixture: 2 (1/4-oz.) envelopes unflavored gelatin • 1 cup cold water • 1/2 cup powdered sugar
Coffee Gelatin: 2 cups strong coffee • Whipped cream   **Wine Gelatin:** 1-1/4 cups red wine • 3 tablespoons honey •
2 to 3 drops cinnamon oil, if desired

1. Soften gelatin in 1/2 cup cold water 5 minutes.

2. In a medium saucepan, dissolve sugar in remaining 1/2 cup water over low heat. Remove from heat.

3. Stir in softened gelatin; stir to dissolve.

4. Strain if mixture is not smooth. Divide gelatin mixture into 2 equal portions. For Coffee Gelatin, add coffee to one portion of the gelatin mixture. Pour into individual glasses. Refrigerate until set. To serve, decorate with whipped cream. Makes 4 to 5 servings.

5. For Wine Gelatin, boil wine with honey until slightly reduced, 3 to 4 minutes. Add cinnamon oil, if desired. Reserve 1/4 cup wine mixture. Blend remaining wine mixture with other portion of gelatin mixture.

6. Ladle into individual molds. Refrigerate until set. To serve, unmold each dessert in an individual dish. Pour reserved wine mixture over each dessert. Makes 3 to 4 servings.

TIP: To make only one type of jelly, use 1/2 the basic gelatin mixture recipe and proceed as directed with desired recipe. Or, to make the full gelatin recipe, double the ingredients for the desired flavor of jelly.

Vanilla Bavarian Cream

2 (1/4-oz.) envelopes unflavored gelatin ● 1/3 cup cold water ● 2-1/4 cups milk ● 3/4 cup granulated sugar ● 6 egg yolks ●
1 teaspoon cornstarch ● 1 tablespoon vanilla sugar, page 192 ● 1 pint whipping cream (2 cups)

1. Lightly oil a 6- to 8-cup mold.

2. Soften gelatin in cold water 5 minutes; place over low heat to dissolve.

3. Heat milk in a saucepan over medium heat.

4. Beat together granulated sugar, egg yolks, cornstarch and vanilla sugar. When milk is very hot, stir gradually into egg-yolk mixture.

5. Return mixture to heat. Cook, stirring constantly, until thickened. Remove from heat. Stir in gelatin mixture.

6. Cool slightly, stirring gently until thickened. Do not beat. The basic cream should not froth.

7. Whip the cream; carefully fold into mixture. Pour into lightly oiled mold. Refrigerate at least 5 hours before serving. Unmold to serve. Makes 6 to 8 servings.

A bavarian is similar in consistency to a cream caramel. A ring mold should be used to ensure that the consistency of the dessert is the same throughout. This classic vanilla bavarian may be used as a basic recipe. Other flavors may be achieved by adding melted chocolate; instant coffee dissolved in a little water; liqueurs or fortified wines, such as Marsala; or fruit, such as strawberries, banana, candied fruit or melon. Fruit-flavored bavarian can be accompanied by mixed, sliced fruit.

Meringues

3 egg whites • 3/4 cup granulated sugar

1. Preheat oven to 225F (105C). Grease a baking sheet. Beat egg whites until soft peaks form.

2. Gradually beat in sugar until stiff peaks form.

3. Spoon mixture in small dollops on a greased baking sheet, or press through a pastry bag with an open nozzle, not using a tip.

4. Bake immediately until firm, about 30 minutes. Makes about 12 meringues.

Meringue generally refers to a sweet made with stiffly beaten egg whites and sugar, cooked in a slow oven until firm. The basic recipe—1/4 cup sugar to each egg white—can be used to make various shapes, including rings, pyramids, pie crusts and nests. Meringue may also serve as a flan base and can be filled with whipped cream, ice cream, custard or fruit. Flavor and color are affected by flavoring added, such as chocolate, coffee and vanilla. Flat meringues arranged in layers with sponge cake, butter cream, fruit and whipped cream, make an elegant and delicious party dessert.

Carrot Halwa

1-1/4 lbs. grated carrots (about 5 cups) ● 2-1/2 cups milk ● 1/2 teaspoon powdered saffron ● 1/4 cup butter ●
1/2 cup powdered sugar ● 2 tablespoons honey ● 1/2 teaspoon ground cinnamon ● 1 (1/4-oz.) envelope unflavored gelatin ●
1/4 cup cold water ● 2 tablespoons chopped almonds, if desired ● 1 banana, thinly sliced, if desired

1. Boil carrots in milk about 1-1/4 hours over low heat until thick and creamy.

2. Add saffron, butter, sugar, honey and cinnamon; stir well. Continue cooking 10 minutes.

3. Soften gelatin in cold water 5 minutes; place over low heat to dissolve. Beat into hot carrot mixture.

4. Pour mixture into 6 (1/2-cup) molds. Refrigerate until firm.

5. To serve, unmold onto serving dishes. Decorate with chopped almonds and banana slices, if desired. Makes 6 (1/2-cup) servings.

Yogurt Gelatin

Gelatin: 1/2 cup powdered sugar ● 1 (8-oz.) carton unflavored yogurt (1 cup) ●
2 tablespoons maraschino or other sweet liqueur ● 1/2 cup whipping cream ● 1 (1/4-oz.) envelope unflavored gelatin ●
1/4 cup cold water **Decoration:** 1 lime, thinly sliced ● Fresh mint leaves

1. Blend sugar and yogurt. Stir in liqueur.

2. Soften gelatin in water 5 minutes; place over low heat to dissolve. Gradually beat dissolved gelatin into yogurt mixture.

3. Whip the cream until stiff. Carefully fold whipped cream into yogurt mixture.

4. Pour mixture into molds.

5. Refrigerate until set.

6. Turn out jellies into individual dishes.

7. Decorate with lime slices and fresh mint leaves. Makes 5 to 6 (1/2-cup) servings.

Cointreau Jellies with Orange Sauce

Cointreau Jelly: 1 (1/4-oz.) envelope unflavored gelatin • 1/4 cup cold water • 1/4 cup sugar • 2 eggs, separated •
1-1/4 cups milk • 3 tablespoons Cointreau or orange juice   **Orange Sauce:** 1/4 cup sugar • 1-1/4 cups orange juice

1. Soften gelatin in cold water 5 minutes; place over low heat to dissolve.

2. Beat together sugar and egg yolks until creamy. Blend in milk. Cook over low heat to thicken.

3. Add dissolved gelatin and liqueur or orange juice.

4. Cool until thickened slightly.

5. Beat egg whites until stiff but not dry.

6. Fold carefully into gelatin mixture.

7. Pour into molds. Refrigerate until firm.

8. Dissolve sugar in orange juice over low heat. Bring to a boil; remove from heat. Allow to cool. To serve, turn out molds onto a serving dish; pour orange sauce around. Makes 6 servings.

Crème de Menthe Mold

1 (1/4-oz.) envelope unflavored gelatin • 2 tablespoons cold water • 3 egg yolks • 3/4 cup powdered sugar •
1 cup warm milk • 1/4 cup crème de menthe • 1/2 cup whipping cream **Decoration:** 6 maraschino cherries

1. Lightly oil a 4-cup fluted mold. Soften gelatin in cold water 5 minutes; place over low heat to dissolve.

2. Beat egg yolks and sugar until creamy.

3. Blend in milk and crème de menthe.

4. Stir in dissolved gelatin. Refrigerate until very thick.

5. Whip the cream until stiff.

6. Fold whipped cream into thickened mint mixture.

7. Pour into mold. Refrigerate until firm.

8. To serve, unmold and decorate with maraschino cherries.

Trifle with Meringue Topping

2-1/2 cups Cream Custard, page 194 • 1 Sponge Cake, page 18 • 1/4 cup fruit juice or fruit-flavored liqueur •
3/4 cup diced candied fruit • 1/4 cup rum • 5 egg whites • 1-1/4 cups powdered sugar • Candied cherries

1. Preheat oven to 350F (175C). Spoon 1/3 of custard into a large round, 8-inch baking dish, 2-1/2 to 3 inches deep.

2. Cut cake into large cubes. Sprinkle with fruit juice or liqueur. Place half of cake pieces in dish over custard.

3. Top with another 1/3 of custard and 1/2 cup candied fruit. Cover with remaining cake cubes. Sprinkle with rum. Top with remaining custard.

4. Beat egg whites until soft peaks form. Gradually beat in sugar until stiff peaks form. Spoon over sponge and custard, covering completely.

5. Decorate with remaining candied fruit and cherries. Bake 3 to 5 minutes until meringue is lightly browned. Makes 6 to 8 servings.

Classic trifle is covered with Chantilly Cream. This is a meringue-topped variation.

Blancmange

1-1/4 cups powdered sugar • 1/2 cup cornstarch • 1-1/4 cups milk • 2 tablespoons white curaçao • 1 cup half and half •
1/2 cup almond milk, see instructions below right • Half and half, if desired

1. Sift sugar and cornstarch into a medium bowl.

2. Add 1/2 cup milk, stirring to dissolve.

3. Heat remaining 3/4 cup milk. Stir into sugar mixture.

4. Stir over low heat until thickened and raw starch taste is gone. This can take up to 30 minutes.

5. Add curaçao and half and half.

6. Stir in almond milk. Pour mixture into individual molds. Refrigerate until set. To serve, unmold. Serve with half and half, if desired. Makes 4 to 5 servings.

Blancmange is a classic French dessert. Basic ingredients are not always identical. Sometimes cream is left out; sometimes no liqueur is used. One essential ingredient, however, is almond milk. It is made by blending 3/4 cup almonds with 1/2 cup water in a blender or food processor. Then squeeze the liquid through a cloth. The blancmange mixture is poured into small molds and refrigerated until set.

Cream-Cheese Mousse

1 (8-oz.) pkg. cream cheese, room temperature • 2 (1/4-oz.) envelopes unflavored gelatin • 3 cups hot milk •
1 teaspoon grated lemon peel • 1/4 cup lemon juice • 1 tablespoon white curaçao or triple sec • 1/2 cup whipped cream •
3 egg whites • 1/2 cup powdered sugar

This light dessert melts in your mouth like ice cream. The recipe given here is not excessively sweet. The sugar can be increased according to individual taste.

Using the same method, flavored mousses can be prepared. Mousses are always very soft in texture and usually have one dominant flavor from which they take their name. Some varieties of mousse are: melon, orange, strawberry, mandarin, pineapple, lemon, pear, peach, pistachio and strawberry. Mousse may also be flavored with liqueur, coffee, cinnamon and wine.

1. Line the base and side of a 9-inch cake pan with waxed paper oiled on both sides or lightly oil a 10-cup ring mold.

2. Beat cream cheese until smooth.

3. Soften gelatin in a little milk. Stir remaining milk into softened gelatin.

4. Gradually stir milk mixture into cream cheese; blend until smooth.

5. Add lemon peel, lemon juice and liqueur. Chill until thick. Then fold in whipped cream. Refrigerate 5 minutes.

6. Beat egg whites until stiff but not dry. Gradually add sugar, beating constantly.

7. Carefully fold whipped egg whites into cream-cheese mixture.

8. Pour into prepared pan. Refrigerate 3 to 4 hours. To serve, unmold onto a cold serving dish.

Chocolate Mousse

4 eggs, separated ● 1/2 cup sugar ● 1/4 cup orange juice or orange liqueur ● 4 oz. semisweet chocolate ●
1/4 cup strong coffee ● 1/4 cup butter ● 1 oz. candied orange peel, if desired ● 1 tablespoon sugar
Decoration: 1 cup whipping cream, lightly whipped

Chocolate mousse differs from all other types of mousse in that
it does not contain the classic ingredients of a mousse—gelatin,
cornstarch or milk. When chocolate is melted and allowed to
cool, it sets the mousse. No other setting agent is needed.

1. In a saucepan, beat together egg yolks and 1/2 cup sugar until thick and pale.

2. Cook over low heat, stirring until thickened. Stir in orange juice or liqueur.

3. Melt chocolate with coffee in a double boiler. Beat in butter until creamy.

4. Stir chocolate mixture into egg mixture.

5. Add orange peel, if desired.

6. Beat egg whites until soft peaks form. Add 1 tablespoon sugar. Beat until stiff peaks form.

7. Stir 1/4 of beaten egg whites into chocolate mixture until well blended. Fold in remaining egg whites.

8. Pour into individual dishes or glasses. Decorate with a layer of whipped cream. Refrigerate until ready to serve.

Cheese Mousse with Blueberries

1/2 cup fresh, frozen or canned blueberries • 2 tablespoons maraschino or kirsch liqueur • 1 teaspoon vanilla sugar, page 192 • 1/2 teaspoon salt • 2 (3-oz.) pkgs. cream cheese, room temperature • 1/2 cup powdered sugar • 1/3 cup whipping cream • 2 tablespoons powdered sugar • 3 egg whites

1. Soak blueberries in liqueur and vanilla sugar.

2. Combine salt and cream cheese; blend until smooth.

3. Stir in 1/2 cup powdered sugar, sprinkling it in gradually through a sieve.

4. Whip the cream, gradually adding 2 tablespoons powdered sugar.

5. Beat egg whites until stiff but not dry.

6. Carefully fold beaten egg whites into whipped cream.

7. Carefully fold this mixture into cream-cheese mixture.

8. Pour mousse into individual dishes.

9. Refrigerate until ready to serve. Decorate each serving with blueberries. Makes 4 to 6 servings.

TIP: Other fruits can be substituted for blueberries.

Vanilla Soufflé

1-3/4 cups milk • 1/2 cup sugar • 1 teaspoon vanilla extract • 1/3 cup all-purpose flour • 1/2 teaspoon salt •
2 tablespoons butter • 5 eggs, separated

1. In a medium saucepan, combine 1-1/4 cups milk, sugar and vanilla. Bring to a simmer. Let stand 15 minutes.

2. Preheat oven to 400F (205C). Butter and sugar 1 large or 6 small soufflé dishes.

3. Stir remaining 1/2 cup milk into flour and salt. Stir this mixture into flavored milk. Bring mixture to a boil, stirring constantly. Stir in butter; cool completely.

4. Beat egg yolks into mixture, 1 at a time. Beat egg whites until stiff but not dry. Carefully fold into flour mixture.

5. Pour mixture into prepared dish or dishes. Dish should not be more than 3/4 full.

6. Place in preheated oven. Immediately reduce oven to 375F (190C). Bake large soufflé 30 to 35 minutes or small soufflés 15 minutes.

Soufflé is a French word that has become an international culinary term. Not only the name, but the recipe or recipes are typical of French cookery. The word itself means "puffed up." Soufflés are frequently savory as well as sweet. This is the basic recipe for sweet soufflés which can be varied by adding chocolate, coffee, vanilla, orange liqueur or fruits, such as oranges, lemons, apricots, strawberries, black cherries, raspberries, peaches, plums or bananas. Puree fruit before adding.

Vanilla Ice Cream

3 cups half and half ● 1 cup sugar ● 4 egg yolks, beaten ● 2 cups whipping cream ● 1 tablespoon vanilla extract

1. In a medium, heavy saucepan, combine half and half, sugar and egg yolks. Stir over low heat until slightly thickened and mixture coats a metal spoon.

2. Cool to room temperature. Stir in whipping cream and vanilla.

3. Freeze in an ice cream maker according to manufacturer's directions. Or, pour into undivided ice trays or loaf pans; cover with foil or plastic wrap. Freeze, stirring 2 or 3 times while freezing. Makes about 3 quarts.

Variation

Coffee Ice Cream: Stir in 2 tablespoons instant coffee powder with egg yolks.

Mint Sherbet & Orange Sherbet

Mint Sherbet: 1 cup chopped mint leaves or 1/2 teaspoon mint extract • 1 cup water • 2/3 cup sugar •
2 tablespoons lemon juice • 1 teaspoon grated lemon peel • Green food coloring, if desired • 2 egg whites
Orange Sherbet: 1-1/4 cups orange juice • 2/3 cup sugar • 2 teaspoons lemon juice • 1 teaspoon grated orange peel •
Orange-flavored liqueur, if desired • 2 egg whites

1. For Mint Sherbet, if using fresh mint leaves, combine mint leaves, water and sugar in a medium saucepan. Bring to a simmer over medium heat; stir until sugar dissolves.

2. Simmer about 5 minutes. Strain liquid; discard mint leaves. Cool to room temperature. If using mint extract, add to water-sugar mixture.

3. Stir in lemon juice, lemon peel and food coloring, if desired.

4. Freeze in an ice cream maker according to manufacturer's directions. Or, pour mixture into undivided ice trays or loaf pans. Cover with foil or plastic wrap. Place in freezer until firm, 3 to 6 hours. Stir 2 or 3 times while freezing.

5. When mixture is almost firm, beat egg whites until stiff but not dry; set aside. Open ice cream maker and fold in egg whites. Or, break up frozen mixture. Process in blender or food processor until smooth but not thawed. Fold in beaten egg whites. Place in freezer.

6. For Orange Sherbet, combine orange juice, sugar, lemon juice, orange peel and liqueur, if desired. Stir until sugar dissolves. Proceed with steps 4, 5 and 6 above.

Lemon Sorbet

4 cups water • 2 cups sugar • 2 teaspoon grated lemon peel • 1-1/4 cups lemon juice

1. In a large saucepan, combine water, sugar and lemon peel. Bring to a boil; stir until sugar dissolves. Reduce heat; simmer about 5 minutes.

2. Cool to room temperature. Stir in lemon juice.

3. Freeze in ice cream maker according to manufacturer's directions. Or, pour into undivided ice trays or loaf pans. Cover with foil or plastic wrap. Place in freezer until firm, 3 to 6 hours.

4. Scrape frozen mixture with a fork until pieces resemble finely crushed ice. Serve immediately.

5. For a smoother texture, process in a blender or food processor. Makes about 2 quarts.

The word *sorbet* comes from Turkish *serbet,* which comes from Arab *sarbat.* In Turkish, the word sherbet refers to a great range of iced drinks with a fruit-juice or fruit-syrup base. These drinks are sometimes thickened with egg white and frozen. Sorbets can be served with a sweet or dry liqueur or champagne.

Dessert Cup

1 qt. red wine   ●   1 qt. sparkling white wine   ●   1 apple, cut in star-shaped slices

1. Combine wines in a punch bowl. Float apple stars on top. Makes 16 (1/2-cup) servings.

No book is complete without at least one beverage. This one is simple, yet unusual and brings to mind other world-famous drinks. Everyone is familiar with *sangria* from Spain, Irish coffee, Mexico's *tequila caliente*—with tequila, lemon juice, soda, grenadine and cassis—and Cuban *libre*—rum, lemon juice and Coca Cola. Russian *kwass* is prepared from dark bread fermented with water, sugar, yeast, raisins and lemon juice. It is sieved before being drunk. Prussian *pillkaller* is a grain spirit that is drunk while holding a slice of liver sausage spread with mustard in the mouth. The sausage is then eaten.

A 17th-century Indian legend links the English word *punch* with the Indian word *punj,* meaning *five.* Punch traditionally contained five ingredients. Indian tea punch does, in fact, contain five ingredients—tea, red wine, rum, orange juice and sugar.

Basic Information

Bain Marie & Double Boiler

The term *bain marie* describes a method of cooking liquid or solid foods in a container placed in boiling water. To make a bain marie, place a saucepan or small baking pan, soufflé dish or ramekins in a baking pan half-full of water. The outer pan should be no more than half-full so no water splashes into the food.

A double boiler is two pans fitted one inside the other. The bottom pan holds water that does not touch the top pan.

Both methods are generally used for cooking sauces, custards and egg dishes, and when melting chocolate. It prevents them from overheating or curdling and keeps them hot. The temperature of the food never reaches the boiling point.

Baking

Oven temperatures are as follows:

Cool	250 to 300F (120 to 150C)
Warm	300 to 325F (150 to 165C)
Moderate	325 to 400F (165 to 205C)
Hot	400 to 450F (205 to 230C)

Always preheat the oven before baking cakes, cookies, soufflés, sweet breads and other desserts unless the recipe calls for a cold oven. Plan your recipe preparation and preheating of the oven so food doesn't have to wait for the oven to heat.

During baking, keep the oven door closed. Opening the door will cause the temperature to drop. Cakes and soufflés, in particular, might be ruined. If it is absolutely unavoidable or if the recipe instructs you to do so, carefully open the door, avoiding a sudden draft of air. Close it as quickly as possible.

Cocoa & Chocolate

Cocoa powder is extracted from fruit seeds of the cocoa plant grown in tropical regions of the world. Each cocoa fruit is 8 to 10 inches long and contains as many as 60 seeds.

The process of extracting cocoa is complicated. Seeds are allowed to ferment in the open air or underground. Then they are washed, dried, roasted and fermented a second time. They are again washed and dried, then they are ground. At this time, cocoa butter is separated from the seeds. Cocoa seeds contain a large quantity of oil and fat that is used in the manufacture of cosmetics, medicines and chocolate.

The major use of cocoa is for the manufacture of chocolate, but it is widely used in pastries, confections and in milk drinks.

Chocolate is manufactured by heating cocoa powder with a good portion of cocoa butter. It is then allowed to set up in various shapes and thicknesses. **To melt chocolate,** grate or break block chocolate into small pieces. Place in top of a double boiler or in a saucepan over or in a pan of simmering water. If the melting chocolate remains thick or develops lumps, add a little margarine—never butter—and reduce the heat. Unused chocolate can be saved, but must be melted again.

Cookies

Cookies are usually sweet and are made with liquid, flour, butter, sugar, eggs and flavorings. Cookies are quite easy to make. Use fresh ingredients, and be sure to measure them carefully. Use baking sheets with very low or no edges. Baking pans with high sides prevent cookies from browning evenly. Bake cookies in the center of the oven if only one baking sheet is being used. If two baking sheets are being used at the same time, leave space between them for air to circulate. Cut cookies the same size to ensure even cooking. Types of cookies include:

Bars are baked in one piece, then cut into slices or squares when cooled.

Dropped cookies are made with dough that is too soft to be rolled with a rolling pin. The dough is spooned onto the baking sheet.

Rolled cookies are flattened with a rolling pin, then cut out with fancy cutters or shaped by hand.

Piped means the dough is piped through a pastry bag, according to the shape desired.

Refrigerator dough is usually rolled into a cylinder and stored in the refrigerator or freezer. When firm, it is sliced or shaped into thin cookies.

Some cookies are sandwiched together with cream cheese, jam, flavored creams or fruit fillings. Tops of cookies may be decorated with chocolate or glacé icing, nuts, candied fruit, jam, granulated or powdered sugar, coconut or other decorative items.

Cookies keep best in an airtight container or in the freezer wrapped in foil. Never put crisp and soft, moist cookies together in the same container. The moisture from the moist cookies will soften crisp cookies.

Equipment

1. **Mortar and pestle** are used to crush toasted nuts, either roughly or into a fine flour. They are also useful for reducing small amounts of foods into a pulp.

2. **Cake pan** suitable for all kinds of cakes. It is available in many sizes.

3. **Small saucepan** with a round bottom and a thick copper base. It is useful for preparing creams and for melting sugar and chocolate.

4. **Dariole mold** for crème caramel and rum babas.

5. **Rectangular fluted mold** for ice creams and iced desserts. The shape simplifies slicing.

6. **Brushes** of various sizes for brushing liqueur onto cakes or for brushing cakes or pastry with egg or melted butter before baking.

7. **Balloon whisk** for hand beating and for whisking egg whites or whipping cream.

8. **Springform pan** for delicate cakes, such as cheesecake, that are difficult to turn out.

9. **Metal scoops** for portions of ice cream or for removing flesh from melons for fruit salads.

10. **Flan pan with fluted edges** and decorated base for tarts and pies.

11. **Metal tubes** for making tubes of flaky pastry.

12. **Hollow metal tubes** for molding and cooking tubes of dough or pastry.

13. **Pastry wheel** for cutting cookies or decorations and for dividing sheets of pastry.

14. **Pastry bag and tips.** This is filled with cream and used for decorating cakes and other sweets. It can also be filled with cookie dough, meringue, icing or caramel.

15. **Ovenproof ramekins** for soufflés, mousses, charlottes and iced desserts.

16. **Cookie cutters** in various shapes and sizes for cutting cookies.

5

Deep-Frying

When deep-frying, use a pan with high sides so the oil will not overflow when food is being cooked.

Recipes often call for moderately hot, hot and very hot fat. These are as follows:

Moderately hot fat uses a low, steady heat to cook food inside before the outside becomes too crisp or begins to burn.

Hot fat has a constant, moderate heat underneath. It is used for sweets that are already partly cooked then coated in batter. The outside is cooked until crisp and golden without overcooking the inside.

Very hot fat uses high heat to cook small pieces of food that must cook rapidly without burning.

After frying one batch of food, let the oil become hot again before adding more food. If the oil is not hot enough, it soaks into the food, making it soggy and preventing a crisp, golden crust.

If you do not have a deep-fat thermometer, use the bread-cube method to determine temperatures. When deep-frying, a 1-inch cube of bread will turn golden brown at these temperatures and times:

345-355F (175-177C)	65 seconds
356-365F (180-185C)	60 seconds
366-375F (186-190C)	50 seconds
376-385F (191-195C)	40 seconds
386-395F (196-200C)	20 seconds

Fruit Juice

To make fruit juice, use fresh fruit that is free from bruises or cut away bruised portions. Cut firm fruit into small pieces. Crush soft fruit. Heat soft fruit with a small amount of water, and firm fruit with enough water to cover. Heat until tender; do not boil. Strain through a damp jelly bag or a fine sieve lined with 3 layers of damp cheesecloth. Squeeze to remove as much juice as possible, then strain again into a pot. Grape juice must be strained again after refrigerating 24 hours.

Meanwhile, prepare a sugar syrup using 3 cups sugar and 4 cups water. Stir over medium heat until sugar dissolves.

Add syrup to juice to taste. Over medium heat, bring to a simmer, 200F (95C). Pour into hot, clean pint, 1-1/2-pint or quart canning jars. Fill to within 1/4 inch of top. Attach lids with self-sealing compound. Process in a boiling-water bath 15 minutes, adding 1 minute for each 1000 feet above sea level. Store in a cool dry place.

Grape juice can also be made by tightly packing washed grapes into hot, clean canning jars, to within 1/2 inch of top. Pour boiling water over grapes to cover. Use a long thin blade or handle to remove air bubbles from jars. Attach lids with self-sealing compound. Process in a boiling-water bath 20 minutes for pints and 25 minutes for 1-1/2 pints and quarts. Add 1 minute for each 1000 feet above sea level. Store in a cool, dry place 2 to 3 months before using.

Fruit Syrup

To make fruit syrup, use fresh fruit of your choice—cherries, strawberries, raspberries, red currants, blackberries, plums, peaches, apricots or grapes. Puree the fruit by crushing with a potato masher, pressing it through a sieve or processing it in a blender. In a heavy saucepan, bring the fruit puree to a boil. Strain through a damp jelly bag or a sieve lined with 3 layers of damp cheesecloth. Let drip at least 2 hours. Squeeze bag or cheesecloth to remove most of juice.

Measure the juice. Add an equal amount of sugar, 1 cup white corn syrup and 1/4 cup lemon juice, if desired. Stirring constantly, bring to a boil over a high heat. Boil 1 minute. Skim foam from surface until surface is clear. Pour into hot, clean 1-pint canning jars to within 1/4 inch of top. Attach lids with self-sealing compound. Process in a boiling-water bath 10 minutes, adding 1 minute for each 1000 feet above sea level. Store in a cool dry place.

Grinding & Toasting Nuts

Almonds, hazelnuts, peanuts and azuki beans can all be ground coarsely or to a fine meal—similar to flour—for use in desserts. When a recipe calls for ground almonds, the nuts should be ground fine, like flour. Use a blender or the fine blade of a food grinder to pulverize the nuts. Remove skins before grinding. Some skins will come off when nuts are rubbed between your hands. **To remove almond skins,** boil 5 minutes in water to cover.

To toast nuts, spread skinless nuts on a baking sheet. Toast in a 350F (175C) oven until browned as desired. Do not let them burn or they will become bitter and unusable. Grind coarsely or finely, as needed for each recipe.

Ice Cream, Sherbet & Sorbet

Basic ingredients of ice cream are sugar, milk or cream, eggs and flavoring, such as vanilla, chocolate, lemon or strawberry. Ice cream is made by blending the ingredients as they freeze or freezing the blended ingredients, then beating to make them smooth and creamy.

Sherbets are frozen combinations of fruit purees, such as pineapple, orange and strawberry, blended with sugar syrup or another sweetener. Gelatin or whipped egg white are sometimes added to give them a light, fluffy texture.

Sorbet is made from fruit puree, juice and sweeteners or may contain wine or liqueur. It contains no milk or eggs, and must be stirred during freezing to reduce the ice crystals. Or, the frozen mixture can be scraped to resemble finely crushed ice.

Icing

Icing is used to cover cakes, breads and rolls. Use a soft icing on breads and rolls so it can be drizzled. When the icing will be spread, it must be soft enough to spread easily before it hardens. Cake icing should be thick so it does not drip.

A very thin icing can be used as a glaze. Spread it over the cake. Let it dry before adding the thicker icing. This keeps crumbs from mixing with the icing. Fruit-based jellies can also be used as glazes.

Leavening Agents

Three different types of leavening agents are used in this book:

Yeast, when combined with flour, moisture and warmth, begins to ferment and converts flour into alcohol and carbon dioxide. These gas bubbles are what leavens bread. Oven heat kills the yeast and causes the gas to expand, raising the bread in a final *oven spring.*

Active dry yeast comes in 1/4-ounce envelopes or in bulk. *Compressed fresh yeast* comes in .06-ounce cakes. One envelope of dry yeast equals 1 scant tablespoon dry yeast or 1 cake compressed fresh yeast.

Active dry yeast has been dehydrated. The cells become active when mixed with a warm liquid. Store dry yeast in a cool, dry place—not in the refrigerator or freezer. Use by the expiration date on the package. Or, *proof the yeast* by combining 1 envelope active dry yeast or 1 cake compressed fresh yeast, 1 teaspoon sugar and 1/4 cup warm water. If the yeast begins to bubble and swell, it is active. If not, discard the yeast and begin with another package.

Compressed fresh yeast must be refrigerated and used within 1 to 2 weeks or by the expiration date on the package. It should always be proofed.

Baking soda or **bicarbonate of soda** reacts when moistened. It is especially volatile when combined with an acid liquid, such as buttermilk. It immediately gives off carbon dioxide. Always blend it with other dry ingredients before it is moistened, then bake as soon as possible.

Baking powder is a combination of baking soda and cream of tartar. *Single-acting* baking powder immediately releases its gas into the batter. *Double-acting* baking powder releases some gas when it is moistened and again when the batter is heated.

To ensure even distribution of baking soda or baking powder and even rising of the dough, blend with other dry ingredients before adding liquid.

Too much baking soda or baking powder gives a baked product a dry, crumbly texture and a bitter taste. It also causes the product to overrise and fall. Too little baking soda or baking powder makes a product heavy and gummy.

Pastry Bag & Decorating Tips

When decorating cakes and desserts with whipped cream, icing or butter cream, use a pastry bag and an assortment of decorating tips. Each tip produces a different patterned effect.

Plain tip has a small round hole for making drops, blobs, dots and for writing and drawing.

Star or pointed tip is used to make stars, rosettes and shells.

Petal tip lets you make decorative scrolls, ribbons and delicate flower designs.

Large drop tip has a large round hole for making large drops, blobs, dots, writing, drawing and for decorating the Gâteau Saint Honoré.

Flower tip is used to make small flowers.

Leaf tip makes delicate leaf and flower designs.

Preserves

Preserve describes several different kinds of products.

Jelly—Clear fruit juice is cooked with sugar to make a gel. Add pectin to juice that doesn't contain enough natural pectin to gel. Jelly will hold its shape when turned out of a mold.

Jam—Whole or chopped fruit is cooked with sugar It is soft enough to spread easily.

Preserve—Whole or large pieces of fruit are suspended in a lightly gelled syrup.

Conserve—Conserve is similar to jam with nuts and raisins added. Chutneys may be conserves with onion, peppers and spices added.

Pickles—This refers to vegetables preserved in brine, oil or vinegar and to spicy chutneys made from fruits and vegetables with added garlic, onion, pepper, mustard and vinegar.

Testing for Doneness

Most desserts are baked a specific amount of time. However, due to variance in oven temperature, it is always wise to test the product to see if it is done. The following are some of the tests that can be made:

Custard: Insert a knife in the center or between the center and side of the dish. If the knife comes out clean—does not have any custard on it—the custard is done. This test is used for individual custards and custard pies.

Bread: Most breads can be tested for doneness by tapping the top with your fingertips. If it sounds hollow, the bread is done. Or, remove the bread from the pan or baking sheet and tap the bottom with your fingertips. If the loaf sounds hollow, it is done *Quick breads and breads containing nuts or fruit* are tested by inserting a wooden pick near the center of the loaf where it will not puncture any fruit or nuts. If it comes out clean and dry, the bread is done. If the bottom of the bread is not as browned as you desire, place the loaf directly on the oven rack. Bake about 5 minutes or to desired brownness.

Cake: Bake minimum time if a range is given before testing doneness. To test most cakes, insert a wooden pick near the center. If the pick comes out clean and dry, the cake is done. If the cake layer is thin, as in a *jelly roll,* press the top with your fingertips. If the surface springs back, the cake is done. At any time, if the cake does not test done, return it to the oven for another 5 to 10 minutes. When done, the cake should pull away from the side of the pan.

Sugar Syrups & Candies

Test	Description	Temperature
Veil	Sugar is dissolved. Syrup runs from spoon in a sheet.	200-215F (95-100C)
Thread	Dropped from a spoon, syrup spins a 2-inch thread.	230-234F (110-112C)
Soft ball Fondant Fudge Penuche	Dropped in very cold water, syrup forms a soft ball that flattens slightly when removed from water. When kneaded, it becomes soft and pliable.	234-240F (112-116C)
Firm ball	Dropped in very cold water, syrup forms a firm ball that does not flatten.	244-248F (118-120C)
Hard ball Divinity	Dropped in very cold water, syrup forms a hard ball.	250-266F (121-130C)
Soft crack Butter-scotch Taffy	Dropped in very cold water, syrup separates into a hard but not brittle thread.	270-290F (132-143C)
Hard crack Brittle	Dropped in very cold water, syrup separates into a hard, brittle thread.	300-310F (149-154C)
Caramel-ized sugar	Syrup turns dark golden, but will turn black at 350F (175C).	310-338F (155-170C)

Caramel is the last stage reached when boiling a sugar syrup. The syrup turns a deep golden brown just before it burns. Caramel is used as a flavoring for desserts, syrups and sauces. Use a small heavy saucepan or skillet with a flat bottom to caramelize sugar. The heavy saucepan ensures even cooking. In a light pan, it will burn in some spots before it browns in others.

If caramelized sugar is used as a flavoring for custard, as with Crème Caramel, after baking, cool completely, then refrigerate at least 2 hours. This lets the caramel soften and take moisture from the custard. When it is turned out, the caramel syrup will come out with the custard. If turned out immediately after cooking, the caramel is still hard and will remain in the mold.

There are two methods of making caramelized sugar. In one, the sugar is melted and browned. In the other, sugar and water are cooked until browned.

To make the first, stirring carefully, heat 1/3 to 1/2 cup granulated sugar over medium heat until the sugar melts and turns golden brown. As the caramelized sugar cools, it becomes hard, so use immediately. Pour into a mold, tipping to distribute evenly. Or, pour boiling water, a little at a time, into the melted, browned sugar to make a syrup. Stir until smooth and all of caramel is dissolved.

Caramel syrup is easily made by boiling 1/2 cup granulated sugar and 1/4 cup water until sugar dissolves. Without stirring, continue boiling until mixture is caramelized. Stirring may cause the syrup to crystallize before it browns. Caramel syrup changes color fast, so watch it carefully. When lightly browned, it is mild and sweet. The darker it becomes, the richer the caramel flavor—unless it burns. Then it is bitter and not usable. Remove from the heat from time to time to control the cooking. When the color is deep golden, dip the base of the pan in cold water to stop cooking immediately. Use to drizzle over fruit, or use in recipes calling for caramelized sugar or caramel syrup.

Liqueur-Sugar Syrup

1-1/2 cups sugar
2 cups water
1 cup liqueur

In a medium saucepan, combine sugar and water. Stir over medium heat until sugar dissolves. Stir in liqueur. Makes about 3 cups.

Vanilla

When a recipe calls for vanilla, it generally means pure vanilla extract that is obtained from the vanilla plant, a member of the orchid family.

Artificial vanilla, which is produced chemically, has a slightly bitter taste. However, artificial vanilla is widely available.

Vanilla Sugar

Vanilla sugar is available in supermarkets and specialty stores, but you can easily make your own. In a 1-pint jar, combine 1-1/2 cups granulated sugar and 1 vanilla bean. Cover tightly. Let stand 1 or 2 weeks before using. Shake jar periodically. As the flavored sugar is used, add more sugar.

Yeast Doughs

Almost any dough can be prepared with yeast, from brioche dough to pizza bases to cakes. For desserts and sweet breads, use low-gluten or all-purpose flour. This will give you a more tender product.

Sugar adds flavor and tenderness to bread, helps to brown the crust and gives a delicate texture. It also helps yeast breads to rise faster.

Salt improves the flavor of yeast doughs. If no salt or less than the recommended amount is used, the flavor will be bland and the dough may rise too quickly. Too much salt will hinder the rising of the dough and may spoil the texture of the final result.

Use warm liquid—usually water, milk or fruit juices. If the recipe includes butter or eggs, the amount of liquid required is less. Sometimes no additional liquid is needed.

Always proof yeast, page 191. Combine proofed yeast with other ingredients as the recipe directs. Beat with an electric mixer or by hand. This initial beating shortens kneading time.

Kneading is important because it develops the gluten strands, making a fine-textured bread. To knead, place the dough on a lightly floured surface.

With lightly floured hands, pick up the dough edge on the side away from you. Fold it toward you. Press down firmly on the dough with the heels of your hands while gently pushing away from you. Turn the dough 1/4 turn. Again pick up the dough on the side away from you, fold it over and press down firmly while pushing away from you. Repeat this action for about 10 minutes until the dough is smooth and elastic.

After kneading, place the dough in a clean, greased bowl. Cover and let rise in a warm place, free from drafts, until doubled in bulk. This may be done by placing the bowl of dough inside another bowl half-full of warm water or placing the dough in an unheated oven. Place a pan of hot water on the shelf below the dough.

Punch down the dough and shape as directed in the recipe. Again, let rise until doubled in bulk. Bake as directed.

If you are making a batter bread, add only enough flour to the yeast mixture to make a stiff batter. Beat well to develop the gluten. Cover and let rise in a warm place, such as over a pan of warm water. Stir down and turn into a prepared pan. Let rise again; bake as directed.

BASIC RECIPES

Marzipan

2-1/4 cups granulated sugar
2/3 cup water
Pinch of cream of tartar
3 cups finely ground, blanched almonds (3/4 lb.)
2 egg whites, beaten stiff but not dry
1/2 to 3/4 cup powdered sugar

Lightly oil a marble slab or baking sheet. Dissolve granulated sugar in water over medium heat. Add cream of tartar; stir until dissolved. Boil without stirring until mixture reaches the soft-ball stage (238F, 115C). Remove from heat. Stir in almonds and beaten egg whites. Return to heat 2 to 3 minutes, stirring constantly. Turn onto oiled marble or baking sheet. Work paste with a spatula 5 to 10 minutes, bringing edges to center. When cool enough to work by hand, knead until smooth. Use powdered sugar, if necessary, to keep paste from sticking. Makes about 2 pounds.

Marzipan can be used to decorate large cakes or it can be made into small marzipan cakes. It can be shaped and colored in a variety of ways, and is often molded into fruit-shapes that can be glazed and colored.

Marzipan and almond paste are similar, and are often confused. Almond paste is used mainly as a filling for cakes and cookies. Marzipan is used mainly for decoration.

Almond Paste

1 lb. almonds
2-1/4 cups granulated sugar
1/4 cup white corn syrup
3/4 cup water
Powdered sugar, if needed

Preheat oven to 350F (175C). Soak almonds in boiling water 5 to 10 minutes or until skins loosen and can be peeled off easily. Peel almonds; place on a baking sheet. Place in oven to dry and toast. Toast only until lightly colored, about 5 minutes. If allowed to burn, almonds cannot be used for almond paste. Grind toasted almonds in batches in a blender or food processor to make a fine flour. Lightly oil a marble slab or baking sheet. In a medium saucepan, dissolve granulated sugar and corn syrup in water. Boil until mixture reaches the soft-ball stage (238F, 115C). While still hot, blend sugar syrup with ground almonds. Pour mixture onto oiled marble or baking sheet. Work with a spatula until mixture is cool enough to handle. Then knead until smooth, dusting with powdered sugar as needed. For immediate use, let paste stand at least 2 hours. Store tightly covered in a cool place. If paste becomes too hard to shape easily, wrap in foil and steam over boiling water until softened. Almond paste can be colored or flavored with liqueurs or extracts. Makes about 2 pounds.

Confectioner's Custard

1 cup plus 2 tablespoons milk
1 cup plus 2 tablespoons half and half
1 teaspoon grated lemon peel or orange peel, or
  1 teaspoon vanilla extract
3/4 cup sugar
1 teaspoon cornstarch
10 egg yolks, beaten

Reserve 1/3 cup milk. In a medium saucepan, combine remaining milk and half and half. Place over low heat. Add lemon or orange peel or vanilla. Gradually add sugar, stirring constantly. Blend reserved 1/3 cup milk with cornstarch. Add to hot milk mixture. Stirring constantly, bring to a boil. Remove from heat. Add 1 cup hot milk mixture slowly to beaten egg yolks. Then add egg-yolk mixture to hot milk mixture, stirring constantly. Return to heat until mixture thickens. Do not overcook. This can be done in a double boiler to prevent overcooking. Makes about 3-1/2 cups.

Cream Custard

1-1/2 cups milk
1/2 cup powdered sugar
1 tablespoon all-purpose flour
1 tablespoon cornstarch
2 egg yolks, beaten
1 tablespoon butter

In a medium saucepan, scald 1 cup milk. In a medium bowl, combine remaining 1/2 cup milk, sugar, flour and cornstarch; stir to blend. Add mixture to scalded milk. Simmer, stirring constantly, until thickened. Add 1/2 to 3/4 cup hot mixture to beaten egg yolks; then add egg-yolk mixture to remaining milk mixture, stirring constantly. Add butter, beating well. Return to heat until mixture simmers. Cool. Makes about 2 cups.

Frangipane Cream

2 egg yolks
1/2 cup sugar
1/4 cup all-purpose flour
1/4 cup finely ground almonds
2 cups milk
Vanilla extract

In a large bowl, beat egg yolks and sugar until pale and creamy. Beat in flour and ground almonds. Gradually stir in milk and vanilla. Place a fine sieve over a medium saucepan. Pour mixture through sieve to remove any lumps. Stir constantly over low heat until thick and smooth. Makes about 3 cups.

Pastry Cream

6 egg yolks
1-1/4 cups powdered sugar
1/2 cup all-purpose flour
2-1/4 cups milk
1 teaspoon vanilla extract or a small piece of
  lemon peel
1 tablespoon butter or margarine

In a medium bowl, beat egg yolks and sugar until pale. While continuing to beat, gradually sift in flour. Gradually add milk. Place over low heat. Add vanilla or lemon peel. Cook, stirring constantly, until mixture has thickened to custard consistency, about 15 minutes. Remove from heat. Discard lemon peel. Melt butter or margarine on surface of pastry cream to prevent a skin from forming while it cools. Makes about 3 cups.

Variations

Zabaglione Pastry Cream: Add 2 to 3 tablespoons dry Marsala.
Chocolate Pastry Cream: Add 2 ounces grated chocolate or unsweetened cocoa powder.

Saint-Honoré Cream

2/3 cup sugar
1/3 cup water
6 egg whites
1 recipe Pastry Cream, above

In a medium saucepan, cook sugar and water to soft-ball stage (238F, 115C). In a medium bowl, beat egg whites until stiff but not dry. Gradually beat in hot sugar syrup. Stir about 1/4 of egg-white mixture into pastry cream. Fold remaining egg-white mixture into pastry cream. Makes about 6 cups.

Variation

Chocolate Saint-Honoré Cream: Gâteau Saint Honoré is sometimes filled and decorated with 2 different-colored creams. They are prepared in the same way. The darker one is made by adding 2 to 4 ounces melted chocolate.

Zabaglione Cream

3 egg yolks
1/2 cup powdered sugar
1/4 cup Marsala or white wine
1-1/4 cups whipping cream

In a medium glass bowl, beat egg yolks and sugar until pale. Beat in wine, 1 tablespoon at a time. Place bowl in a bain marie over low heat. Beat with a whisk until mixture is light and fluffy. Cool, stirring occasionally. Beat whipping cream until stiff. Carefully fold into cooked mixture. Makes about 4 cups.

Chantilly Cream

2 cups whipping cream
2 to 4 tablespoons powdered sugar

In a large bowl, whip cream until soft peaks form. Beat in sugar to taste until stiff peaks form. Makes about 3-1/2 cups.

Chantilly Cream is sweetened whipped cream. Unsweetened whipped cream and whipped cream with sugar and vanilla extract added are sometimes incorrectly called Chantilly Cream. In spite of extensive research, no one knows where or when the name originated. Chantilly is a town in northern France, famous for lace and pottery. The invention of sweetened whipped cream is often attributed to chef Vatel, who spent many years at Château de Chantilly. Some maintain that it was invented by Sicilian pastry chef, Procopio dei Coltelli. Both lived during the 17th century. Another theory is that the name Chantilly was first used in Rome when French troops from Chantilly were occupying the town.

Fondant Icing

1-1/2 cups sugar
1/2 teaspoon cream of tartar
3/4 cup water

In a large, heavy saucepan, combine sugar and cream of tartar. Stir in water. Stir over low heat until sugar dissolves. Cover and bring to a boil. Remove cover; boil until mixture reaches soft-ball stage (238F, 115C). Cool to room temperature. Beat vigorously with a wooden spoon until white and creamy. Use immediately to ice a cake. If fondant becomes too stiff to spread, add a little hot water, then beat until smooth. Makes about 2 cups.

Butter Cream

3/4 cup plus 2 tablespoons butter or margarine
1 cup powdered sugar
4 egg yolks
2 egg whites, if desired

In a medium bowl, cream butter or margarine and sugar until light and fluffy. Beat in egg yolks, 1 at a time. Whisk egg whites until stiff but not dry. Gently fold beaten egg whites into butter mixture. Makes about 2-1/2 cups.

Variations

Vanilla Butter Cream: Beat in 1-1/2 teaspoons vanilla extract with egg yolks.
Liqueur Butter Cream: Beat in 2 tablespoons liqueur of choice with egg yolks.
Hazelnut Butter Cream: After folding in beaten egg whites, fold in 1/2 cup ground toasted hazelnuts.
Pistachio or Almond Butter Cream: After folding in beaten egg whites, fold in 1/4 to 1/2 cup finely chopped or ground pistachios or almonds.
Lemon Butter Cream: Beat in 2 tablespoons lemon juice with egg yolks.
Chocolate Butter Cream: Beat in 2 ounces melted unsweetened chocolate with egg yolks.
Coffee Butter Cream: Beat in 2 teaspoons instant coffee powder with egg yolks.
Pistachio Grand Marnier Butter Cream: Beat in 2 tablespoons Grand Marnier with egg yolks. After folding in beaten egg whites, fold in 1/4 cup finely chopped or ground pistachios.

Glacé Icing

2 cups powdered sugar
3 to 5 tablespoons hot water

Sieve powdered sugar into a large bowl. Powdered sugar should always be sieved before making icing. Stir in water, a little at a time, until mixture forms a thick smooth paste of coating consistency.

Variations

Add any of the following flavorings: cocoa powder, chocolate, coffee, Grand Marnier or other liqueurs, orange, lemon, caramel, cream cheese, strawberry, cherry, milk, fruit juice, almond extract, rose water or vanilla extract. Icing can also be tinted any desired color.

Weeping Icing: Add more water so mixture is thinner. This is often used on babas.
Royal Icing: In place of water, use 1 egg white for each 1-1/2 cups powdered sugar. Lightly beat egg white. Sift sugar as it is gradually stirred into egg white. Add a few drops of lemon juice to make icing whiter. Icing is ready when it will stand up in peaks. Store in a glass container. To use again, heat gently; add a few drops of water, if necessary.

Sponge Cake

6 eggs, separated
3/4 cup sugar
1-1/2 cups cake flour, sifted
1/4 teaspoon vanilla extract

Preheat oven to 325F (165C). Grease and lightly flour an 8- or 10-inch springform pan. In a medium bowl, beat egg yolks with sugar and vanilla until light and fluffy. Beat egg whites until stiff but not dry; fold carefully into egg mixture. Fold in flour. Pour batter into prepared pan. Bake 10-inch cake 40 minutes or 8-inch cake 45 minutes or until cake tests done. An 8-inch cake can be split into 3 layers. A 10-inch cake can be split into 2 layers. Makes 1 (8- or 10-inch) cake.

Caramelized Fruit

2/3 cup sugar
1/3 cup water
Fruit of your choice

In a small saucepan, cook sugar and water until light brown. Dip fruit in caramelized sugar. Let harden, then dip in caramelized sugar again. Makes about 1/3 cup.

Fresh and dried fruit can be caramelized by dipping them in caramelized sugar once, allowing the sugar to harden, and then dipping the fruit in the caramelized sugar again. Candied fruit and citrus peel can also be caramelized. These can be sandwiched together with a marzipan filling before being caramelized.

Glazes

Honey Glaze: Melt honey over low heat with a few spoonfuls of water.
Honey Glaze with Liqueur: To the above add a few drops of liqueur. Stir until blended and slightly reduced. The spirit most often used is rum. White rum gives a pale glaze while dark rum results in a dark glaze.
Jam Glaze: Melt a few tablespoons of jam over low heat. The jam will become more liquid and will be easy to brush while still warm. For a thinner glaze, dilute jam with a little water. The jams most frequently used in baking are apricot, which gives a golden glaze, and raspberry, which gives a reddish glaze. Fruit jelly can also be used as a glaze in the same way.
Rum Glaze: Melt powdered sugar with a little rum in a saucepan over low heat. Stir to blend. Use 1 to 2 tablespoons rum per 1 cup powdered sugar.

Sweet Shortcrust Pastry

1-3/4 cups all-purpose flour
1/2 cup sugar
1/2 teaspoon salt
1/2 cup butter
2 eggs, slightly beaten
1 teaspoon grated lemon peel or
  1/8 teaspoon vanilla extract

This sweet shortcrust pastry is the basic recipe on which there are several variations. Cocoa powder, ground almonds or hazelnuts can be added. Shortcrust pastry should be prepared as quickly as possible, otherwise it crumbles when rolled out.

In a medium bowl, combine flour, sugar and salt. Make a well in center. Work in butter. Add eggs and lemon peel or vanilla. Blend all ingredients together until a smooth ball of pastry is formed. Press pastry in bottom and side of pan. Or, refrigerate 30 minutes. Then roll pastry to desired size. Bake at 450F (230C) 10 to 12 minutes. Bake tarts or tartlets at 375F (190C) 15 to 20 minutes or until golden brown.

Quantities given here are sufficient for a 9-inch flan pan, a 7-inch pie pan, 8 (3-1/2-inch) tarts or 20 tartlets.

Puff Pastry & Flaky Pastry

4 cups all-purpose flour
1 teaspoon salt
2 cups butter, room temperature
1/4 to 1/2 cup cold water or dry white wine
1 beaten egg for glaze
Sugar

In a large bowl, combine flour and salt. Work 1 cup butter into flour. Stir in enough water or wine to make a dough. Roll out dough with a rolling pin to a rectangle 3 times as long as it is wide. Spread remaining butter across 2/3 of surface. Fold dough into thirds, making sure that the unbuttered third is in the middle. Press edges together with the rolling pin or by hand to prevent butter from squeezing out. Roll out pastry into a rectangle as before. Fold in thirds again. Wrap in plastic wrap. Refrigerate 30 minutes. Repeat this process twice for quick flaky pastry or 5 times for genuine puff pastry. Preheat oven to 425F (220C). Butter a rectangular baking sheet. Dust with sugar. Roll pastry to desired shape; place on prepared baking sheet. Brush with beaten egg; dust with sugar. Bake 15 minutes or until lightly browned.

INDEX

Photo Credits

Maki Irie: 13, 28, 180
Ai Kidosaki: 14, 26, 37, 42, 43, 60, 63, 64, 66, 79, 84, 85, 92, 122, 133, 169
Katsumi Sakaguchi: 16, 17, 18, 24, 34, 36, 38, 45, 46, 72, 80, 120, 158
Masako Hamano: 20
Fusako Holthaus: 87, 88, 178, 184
Aiko Ochiai: 90, 118, 172, 185
Nobuko Shimizu: 168
Reiko Kasai: 48, 117, 124, 126
Minako Imada: 65, 69, 115
Hisashi Kudo: 52, 86, 163, 165, 170, 175, 176, 182, 183
Merry Minami: 131, 135, 136, 140, 141, 142, 144, 146, 148, 149, 150, 155, 156, 160
Tokiko Suzuki: 95, 97, 98, 100, 102, 103, 104
Eisei Shin: 105, 106, 109, 110
Mario Rossi, Milan: 22, 23, 27, 30, 31, 32, 33, 49, 50, 51, 57, 58, 61, 68, 70, 76, 89, 113, 128, 134, 166, 167, 173, 181
Roberto Circia & Giorgio Perego, Vimodrone (Milan): 188, 189

Thanks to Eugenio Medagliani for supplying the utensils for the photograph on pages 188-189.

7.42390353821

Printed and bound in Italy by Arnoldo Mondadori Editore, Verona